Revealing Your hidden Horse

A Revolutionary Approach to Understanding Your Horse

by Mark Hanson

Whether your horse is "good" or "bad;" whether he lives a long, fulfilled, happy life or a life of misery and pain, sickness, disease and suffering; whether he is your best equine friend or your worst equine nightmare; all will depend on only two things: **what you believe about him and the environment you create for him.**

Insanity:

Doing the same thing over and over again

and expecting different results.

—Albert Einstein

ISBN 978-1-4476-7827-4

Hanson, Mark, 2011

Revealing Your Hidden Horse:
A Revolutionary Approach to Understanding Your Horse

First Edition 2011

Dedication

To my daughter Lucy.
Without your persistence
and dedication to the cause
of having your own horse,
none of this would have happened.
Thank you.

Acknowledgements

When I first started writing and putting my thoughts down in notebooks, I assumed in my innocence that authors simply presented a perfectly finished manuscript (with no typos) to a publisher and that was that—a new book is born. Little did I know.

Books it seems are never just the vision or passion of one person. They are the result of a team of people collaborating, in this case, through the magic of the internet, from all over the world. So I would like to thank all those good folk who have read my erratic ramblings over the last few years, and been nice enough to say kind things about them. Those who gave up their time to read some of the early versions of the book and especially those brave folk who put up with strange (but nevertheless quite correct), British spellings and didn't complain.

I would especially like to acknowledge the work of one person, Michelle Twohig, who despite living more than one ocean and an entire continent away—and thus a bizarre eight hours in the past—has been the driving force behind this book. She has been my editor, designer, occasional inspiration and guide through this process. Without her this book would not exist.

Thank you, Michelle.

Contents

Introduction 1

Part One
The Past, the Present...and the Truth 3

Chapter 1
The Truth About Horses 5
The start of the journey 6
Why do we need to understand this relationship? 7
The horse-human equation 10
What is a horse? 10
The horse is a prey animal 11
The human is a predator animal 11
The horse is a foraging animal 13
The horse is a traveling animal—a creature of movement 14
Silent sufferers 14
Summary Chapter 1: The Truth About Horses 14

Chapter 2
The Laws of Behavior and Their Consequences 17
Reinforcement..19
Positive Reinforcement 20
Negative Reinforcement 20
Positive Punishment 20
Negative Punishment 21
Summary of the laws of behavior 21
The coercion test..21
Horses and threats 22

Flight 23
Fight 23
Compliance 23
Minimal effort 24
More compliance 25
Stress 25
Laws of coercion 27
Coercion is always positively reinforcing for the coercer 27
Do horses use coercion? 28
Coercion always generates more coercion 28
Coercion generates counter coercion 29
The laws of behavior and us 30
Coercion and culture 31
Summary Chapter 2: The Laws of Behavior and Their Consequences 31

Chapter 3
The Four Models of Horsemanship 33
The Utility Model 34
Control 37
Uniforms and uniformity 37
The Utility Model and other cultures 38
The Utility Model and tools 39
Practical and efficient 39
The Utility Model and professionals 39
Bandage solutions 41
Superstition 41
The Utility Model and the media 42
The Utility Model is a masculine model 43
The Utility Model and money 43
The Utility Model has a high fallout rate 44
Utility Model limitations 44
Summary of Chapter 3: The Utility Model 45

Chapter 4
The Anthropomorphic Model 47
So how did all this start? 48
So what is anthropomorphism? 48
The first rule of anthropomorphism 49
The second rule of anthropomorphism 50
The third rule of anthropomorphism 51
The fourth rule of anthropomorphism 51

Horses and stables 52
How owners cope with this situation 53
Treats and "stuff" 53
The four big superstitions 55
Diet 56
What is anthropomorphism, really? 58
The terrible secret 59
Some science 61
How horses cope with stress 62
Depression and stress 64
Anthropomorphism is a feminine idea 65
Anthropomorphism and money 65
Summary Chapter 4: The Anthropomorphic Model 66

Chapter 5
The Natural Horsemanship Model 69
Natural horsemanship systems 69
Back to school...70
You're in the army now... 71
Systems and negative reinforcement 72
Confusion 73
Phases of pressure and yielding to pressure 73
Why natural horsemanship? 75
Natural horsemanship is based on controlling horse behavior 76
So what is the advantage of this behavior to horses? 76
Negative reinforcement as communication not control 77
Where natural horsemanship gets it wrong.........................77
Natural horsemanship is similar to hunting 78
GOAL! 79
Isolate your target 79
Stalking phase...79
Success 79
Training 80
GOAL! 80
Isolate your target 80
Stalking phase...80
Success and riding 81
Power, control and money 81
Leadership 81
Natural horsemanship is a masculine model 84
A negative world..85

Summary Chapter 5: The Natural Horsemanship Model 86

Chapter 6
Diet 89
Our part in this "horse-human equation" 90
A better way 93
Cereals and sugar 94
Tricks and treats 95
Dysbiosis or leaky gut syndrome 98
Summary Chapter 6: Diet 100

Part Two
The Good Stuff 103

Chapter 7
The Natural Horse Keeping Model 105
Not wild horses—natural horses 106
Seven principles of Natural Horse Keeping 106
Real natural horsemanship 108
Prey animal intelligence 113
The last principle 114
Housing versus life in a herd 116
Clothing versus freedom of choice and shelter 116
It should be obvious but horses do not wear clothes 117
Is blanketing always bad? 119
Clipping horses 122
Horseshoes versus movement 123
Horseshoes are the ultimate bandage solution 124
Diet in natural horse keeping 127
Long fiber 128
Summary Chapter 7: The Natural Horse Keeping Model 130

Chapter 8
The Environment 133
Environments and "needs" 133
The home range 133
Personal needs 134
Social/herd needs 135
Nutritionally rich and nutritionally poor environments 138
Nutritionally rich environments 139
Individual needs: personal safety 140

Detection and movement 140
Grazing and drinking 141
Rest and sleep 141
Body care 142
Temperature regulation 143
Minerals, vitamins and self-medication 143
Hooves and movement 143
Collective needs of the herd: permanence 144
Copying or modeling 144
Play 145
Territory and exploration 146
On track 147
Summary Chapter 8: The Environment 147

Chapter 9
What Is a Track System? 149
Movement on track 149
Feeding a fiber-based diet on track 150
Socializing on track... 150
Self-grooming and self-medicating on track 150
Barefoot horses on track 150
Self-renewing system 151
Track systems are good for the environment 151
Health 152
Summary Chapter 9: What Is a Track System? 152

Chapter 10
Control and Communication 155
Martingales 156
Pressure 157
Whips and spurs 158
Conventional training is based on our hunting instincts.................... 158
Anthropomorphic tools 158
Merged training methods 159
Breeding 159
Communication 160
The fundamentals of positive reinforcement training (PRT) 160
Classical conditioning.. 161
Operant conditioning 161
The difference between a treat and a reward 162
Stuff! 162

Rewards 163
Positive reinforcement is not a system 163
Right behaviors and "wrong" behaviors 163
Extinction 164
Natural horsemanship tools.. 164
Positive reinforcement tools 165
Optional tools in natural horse keeping 166
Treeless saddles 166
Training areas 167
Clicker training is remembered 167
Increasing pressures versus refinement 168
Four phases of positive reinforcement (refinement) 169
The four laws of learning 170
The first law: linking 170
The second law: repeating 170
The third law: generalizing... 171
The fourth law: maintaining 172
More techniques 172
Variable reinforcement 173
Summary Chapter 10: Control and Communication 174

Chapter 11
Positive Reinforcement Training and Relationships 176
Building the bridge of trust... 179
Respect 180
How to clicker train a horse 181
Dogs and dolphins 182
The first steps... 184
Copying or modeling 185
Summary Chapter 11: Positive Reinforcement Training and Relationships 187

Chapter 12
Great Questions, Great Answers 189
The emotion of compassion 189
Sympathy or empathy... 189
Compassion leads the way 190
Compassion + Empathy = Natural Horse Keeping 190
Final thoughts 192

About
Mark Hanson... 195

Introduction

There is no big secret to understanding horses. All it takes is an extreme amount of common sense, a lifetime of knowledge and the willingness to see the horse as a horse.

I wrote this book for everyone who wants to truly understand horses. I deliberately did not set out to write a science book neither did I write it entirely for adults. My idea was that this book, although containing many scientific references and terms, should still be something any child of 12 or 13 years of age should be able to pick up, read and understand. I wanted this simplicity of approach because in the horse world, or rather the human world as it relates to horses, confused ideas abound. In most of the books and courses based on traditional approaches to horses developed prior to and within the 20th century (including methods known as "natural horsemanship"), you will find a great deal of well-meaning yet unscientific misinformation.

Important:

I recommend that you read this book from beginning to end since the information in it is presented logically. Each piece builds upon the science and principles of those before it. I give many examples, using my own horses and my own management in some of them to make the point. If an item is important enough I will repeat it, as this book is intended to be a process of learning and enlightenment.

In this book you will discover your "hidden horse" as the one you define within. You will come to understand that your definition determines your gift as a 21st century horse whisperer with a natural and intuitive understanding of horses. People who appear to have this gift do not rely on "magic" but on an extreme form of common sense to which they have added a deep understanding of the horse from the perspective of the species, rather than how humans tend to portray and see them. This ability is routinely challenged (sometimes daily) as human desires and agendas conflict with the needs of the horse—even causing some popular horse whisperers to bend to the pressure. My hope is that this book will give you the knowledge and understanding you need to look at horses in a new way, reveal your hidden horse as you become a true horse whisperer, and guide you in making your decisions when (not if) human desires and the needs of horses conflict.

1

Part One

The Past, the Present. . .and the Truth

There really is a hidden horse inside our horses.

It is sometimes a little strange,

always rather wonderful,

and it is waiting for you to discover it.

The 20th century model of

horse training and horse keeping

is about to evolve.

Chapter 1
The Truth About Horses

I have always been fascinated by how humans behave when they are around animals. I suppose it goes back to my childhood when my father was a vet and our home was above a busy London veterinary hospital with a daily stream of animals and their owners—each case with a story to tell.

I can't remember when I first began to wonder why humans did the things they did to animals—perhaps it was a result of being exposed, at too young an age, to tragic cases of animal (and human) suffering, or perhaps it was the many wonderful occasions when the relationship between human and animal led to a positive and happy outcome. It may have been a mixture of both of these things, but I do know that everything came together in my young life when I met my first horse. However...

No sooner had I discovered this wonderful animal that was to play such a large part in my life, than I realized horses were treated differently for some strange reason.

As I got to know more about the horse world, and as I got to observe more horses and more humans together, I found the relationship between our two species a deeply complex one and frequently very strange. It seemed nobody had a clear idea of what kind of animal a horse actually was, and if they did, that definition depended largely on what they wanted from it. Consequently, I realized most relationships between horses and humans were highly unbalanced and based firmly on what benefited the human. Very rarely was it based on what the horse wanted or needed. I was also puzzled at the double standards that were frequently applied to the horse, yet seldom applied to other species. For example, why is it highly unlikely that someone would trade in the family cat yet it is quite acceptable to trade in the family horse? Even more puzzling: Why is it perfectly "normal" (and legal) to carry and use a whip "to encourage" a horse, but the same treatment used on a dog could land you in court?

After a while I also realized that strangest of all, certain people who really liked horses and were frequently knowledgeable and experienced owners, took actions that put them *in direct conflict with their horse*. Whereas they wanted nothing more than a peaceful, happy and cooperative relationship, they found instead, that every day they were fighting against their horse and their relationship was becoming increasingly unsatisfactory, frustrating and even potentially dangerous. What, I wondered, was going wrong?

The start of the journey

To find the answers to these questions and a thousand like them, I began to study. I started to read and learn from the works of the great horsemen and women of history. I studied horse masters, the dressage masters, the horse whisperers and natural horsemen from around the world and most of all I started my own herd of horses. These were horses I could study and observe *as horses* without the interference of the ideas of my fellow human beings about what was the "right" or "wrong" way of doing things.

I wondered if there was some universal truth or ability the horse masters of history all possessed and I quickly found there was. It was both simple and obvious and each and every natural "animal person" possesses it. All this study gave me the world of the traditional and historical view of horses and even a bit of "animal magic," but I knew there must be more. I turned my attention to the other side—the scientists.

I studied, and continue to study, the work of behaviorists, ethologists, zoologists, nutritionists and vets to see whether there were adequate *scientific explanations* for the behaviors I had witnessed in my own horses and observed as anecdotes in the stories of the horse masters. I learned—especially from the field of behaviorism—the idea of common universal principles and laws of behavior, and I realized these applied not only to animals, but also to human behavior as well. Gradually I began to build up a picture of the relationship between the horse and human being.

Sadly I realized that with few rare exceptions this relationship was not a happy one. Even though I tried to take a balanced view by drawing on many sources, the picture I was building proved over and over again to be highly unbalanced and *always in favor of the human being.*

However, there were also rewards from this work. By coming to understand the real nature of the horse, I was able to develop relationships with my own horses based on what I considered worthwhile principles such as mutual trust, respect, loyalty and cooperation.

> Before we go further I think it is important to make the point that I am not someone who regards the horse (or any other animal), as a "cute" creature that must be protected from nasty human beings who would do it harm. My attitude toward horses is one of **total respect** for the horse as an animal **in its own right**. I consider this to be the only really healthy way to think of any animal. Any other mindset toward the horse is not only disrespectful, it is potentially dangerous.

Why do we need to understand this relationship?

The horse has been our companion for only a few thousand years, yet in that relatively short time we have traveled far together. Horses and humans have explored the planet, created empires and built many civilizations, yet ever since the first encounter between our two species, we have always tended to look at the horse for what we can get out of it. At first we saw it as a food source, then as transport, and lastly as the forerunner of so many of the jobs now done by machinery. However, in the last fifty years the role of the horse has been changing. Most of the mechanical roles filled by horses have ended, to be replaced by the combustion engine and the electric motor. The horse has become an animal largely fulfilling the role in our lives of leisure and pleasure. And that, as always, means *our* leisure and *our* pleasure.

But something is also going very wrong....

It is a bit like the human who, after many years of faithful service, is retired and finds he has time on his hands. However, like many human interpretations of horse behavior, this is wrong. The horse has not retired because the horse was never a willing partner in our work. The horse was what he always was— just a horse—nothing more and nothing less. He never understood why he should carry us thousands of miles in the direction only we wanted to go and he never understood the murderous hatred and terror behind our wars. All he wanted, all he ever wanted, was to return to his herd and graze in the peaceful company of other horses.

But this is exactly what he has *not* been able to do, and this is taking its toll on his health, safety, and lifespan. Horses are living increasingly shorter lives and, I believe, lives in which they are sicker, in more pain, and frequently under the daily influence of enforced drugs for long periods of time. I believe also that what we have done to horses in the last fifty years has produced a greater threat to the health and well-being of the horse as a species than anything that went before. This is why—before it is too late—we need to understand the implications of what we are doing to "post-industrial" horses on a global scale. We need to understand how our ideas and the reality of the horse are moving apart, and the best place to start this is to begin with an understanding of the evolution of the relationship between our two species.

If we do not clearly understand our relationship with the horse, we cannot understand how to make things better. Neither can we recognize when we *need* to make things better. If we only base our relationship on traditional knowledge and the existing systems of the past, we will find we are unable to take advantage of new discoveries and new thinking. If we look to our relationships with other species, we find that horses are being left behind. Furthermore it seems we often reserve a particularly harsh set of beliefs for the horse that we would find wholly unacceptable as treatment for a dog.

New ideas about dog psychology, breeding and training based on viewing the dog as a member of a pack are leading to happier and healthier dogs as well as happier, healthier owners. In the world of exotic animals and zoos—traditionally based on displaying animals for public amusement—science and the need to preserve captive species has led to breakthroughs in the way we keep captive wild animals. We now acknowledge the need to provide interesting, stimulating environments that mimic their natural environments. In agriculture there is a growing movement away from intensive factory farming methods, and because the perceptions of the general public are changing, a more liberal approach now bases animal welfare on management systems inspired by the natural behavior of the animal rather than the unsophisticated exploitation of them as units of food production that simply require minimal food, water and shelter.

But these trends in modern thinking are *almost never applied to horses*. Instead there is considerable resistance to the idea that the way we manage horses needs to change at all, despite the fact that most management methods are based on a traditional model dating back several hundred, if not thousands of years!

Although developments have been made in training methods such as "natural horsemanship," these systems are useful but tend to focus on what we can do *to* the horse and very few of them address the overall question of how we look after the horses in our care and what our attitude to them should be. *Real* natural horsemanship should be a *holistic* approach that covers not only how we train our horses, but also how we manage every aspect of horse keeping. It seems hypocritical to adopt the principle of training a horse in a "natural" way while keeping the horse in a management system based entirely on historical tradition and human convenience.

True natural horsemanship should encompass every aspect of the horse as an animal. It should be based on providing a stimulating environment

- in which the horse can show most, if not all, of its natural horse behavior,
- in which it can interact naturally with other horses in a herd environment, and
- in which it can exercise its right to flight and movement if it needs to do that.

It should be based on a diet founded on the way the horse's digestive system works, not on anthropomorphic, human ideas about mealtimes and treats. Once we have addressed these issues, and many others that you will discover in this book, we can begin to look at our interactions with the horse and start to apply new and better ways of relating to our horses. This will then give us a truly balanced view of what we are doing when we become the owner of a horse.

The following statement is the essence of what this book is all about:

Whether your horse is "good" or "bad"; whether he lives a long, fulfilled, happy life or a life of misery and pain, sickness, disease and suffering; whether he is your best equine friend or your worst equine nightmare; all will depend on only two things: **what you believe about him and the environment you put him in**.

In the next few chapters we will look at how many beliefs about horses are not in their best interest. By the end of this book I hope to change your understanding, and possibly many of your own beliefs. If I can change your understanding, I am confident it will create in your mind a new set of beliefs and ideas about your horse that will help change the world of horses for good.

So here is a taste of the knowledge to come:

- **The four laws of behavior**. These are four universal laws that work not only on the trainee but also on the trainer at the same time. When you can understand these simple concepts you will understand why things work and why they don't.

- Certain aspects of the four laws are based on a principle called **coercion** which comes with common side-effects. I will explain to you what they are, how they work, and what the consequences are.

- I will discuss the way humans think about horses and I will introduce the idea of **the four models of horsemanship.** The first two models are about how we think about the horse traditionally and how we often misinterpret the behavior of the horse in a way that suits our own emotions. It is important that we realize what we are doing when we apply these models of thinking.

- The third model deals with something different—the "system thinking" found within many of the currently popular **Natural Horsemanship** techniques. I will examine where their weaknesses lie, even though some of these systems are a step in the right direction.

- The fourth and last model is something quite new and positive, and we are just scratching the surface of the potential of this model of thinking. I call it the **natural horse keeping model**.

But before we get into the whys and wherefores of the relationship between horses and humans, we first have to understand the true nature of these two species.

The horse-human equation

The horse-human equation starts our journey with the most basic question of all:

What is a horse?

Although this is the simplest of questions, it is often something those who have spent a lifetime with horses do not consider. Even career equine professionals often do not understand the implications of the answer to this question. Of all the things a horse owner must understand about a horse **THIS IS THE MOST IMPORTANT.** It is the key to understanding everything your horse does; it is the key to your relationship; it is the key to a long happy and healthy life for you and your horse. It is, quite simply, the key to everything.

> Without a thorough understanding of this fact and all the things it implies, you are building your equestrian knowledge on a complete misunderstanding in which little or nothing you do to your horse will make any sense to it.

So here it is, the secret behind every true horse whisperer, behind all natural horsemanship, behind all the ancient wisdom of the horse masters throughout history, ethology, behavioral science, and a great deal of modern veterinary science. It is simply six words:

The horse is a prey animal

If you remember nothing else about the horse from this book, *remember this simple truth.*

If you do, and you keep this thought in the front of your mind when dealing with horses the "lights will come on." Suddenly you will see the why behind the outcomes, the cause behind the effects.

Of course, this is only half of the truth of the horse-human equation as equations must be balanced. Here is the second part:

The human is a predator animal

This means that humans and horses are *opposites* in almost every way. It means that humans and horses are programmed by nature to continually think up ways of doing the opposite of what the other one wants. For example, horses are *flight* animals *because* they are prey animals. This means their primary defense from predators is to run away. Humans on the other hand see this ability to run away as the first thing that must be *controlled*, so we build pens and corrals; we put head-collars, ropes and bridles on them; and when we ride them we use bits of metal in their mouths to keep them from running away.

When we realize the idea that horses are our opposites, a lot of what they do suddenly becomes clear. When we view horses as prey animals, we can understand why they are so sensitive, why they see much more than we can, hear much better than we can, and detect more things by smell than we can. All this is because a prey animal has to be 100% tuned into its environment in order to detect anything that might be a threat or prove to be dangerous.

> This is why horses are so famously spooked by things that we think are ridiculous, such as a rustling piece of paper or a plastic bag. The trouble is, we humans love to interpret how our horse is behaving and of course, we do this from our perspective as predators. To us it seems ridiculous to be afraid of something like a piece of flapping plastic, but to a horse it makes perfect sense. Usually we interpret this by thinking that the horse is being stupid to behave in this way when in fact, from a prey animal's point of view, it is behaving extremely intelligently.

It makes a lot of sense for a prey animal to have super-senses tuned into the environment to detect as quickly as possible anything that might be a threat—*before it can attack them*—then, to react as quickly as possible as a flight animal to get far enough away to be safe enough to turn around and assess the threat from a distance. By behaving in this way horses have learned to survive.

Learning from a distance is a lot better than learning by experience if you are a prey animal. This wise old saying puts it well:

> If you are a predator and you make a mistake, you might *miss* your breakfast. However, if you are a prey animal and you make a mistake, you *are* breakfast!

So, now we know two things about the horse—prey and flight animal—that we may not have fully appreciated before. What else can we discover about the horse?

A horse is a herd animal

This idea stems from the fact that the horse is a prey animal. The horse is a herd animal *because* it is a prey animal. But why do horses live in herds?

- A herd keeps them safe.

And the most motivating *emotion* in the world to a prey animal is the *need to feel safe.* From this we can discover:

- The presence of other horses allows a horse to feel safe.

If prey and predator animals are opposites, we must consider how we usually treat a horse. After we take away its power of flight, we usually attempt to isolate it from the herd by putting it in a some sort of pen or we take it away from the herd so we can do things to it, such as groom it or tack it up and go for a ride. By far and away the most popular way of isolating a horse is to trap it in a stable. I make no apology for using the expression"trap."It may not be what we intend, but it is certainly what we are doing from a prey animal's point of view—which is of course, the opposite of a human point of view.

> Ironically, if you ask most people why they put horses in stables they will say because they want to keep the horse safe and protected but as we have seen, by isolating the horse from the herd we are actually doing the opposite of what allows a horse to feel safe and protected. We are trapping and isolating it when all the horse really wants is to return to the herd and the presence of other horses.

As I will show later in the book, the main reason we keep horses in stables is not for their protection as much as for our good feelings, but more about that later.

There is one more big, general point we can make about the horse and it is closely linked to this idea of giving the human being good feelings and it is to realize that:

The horse is a foraging animal

In the wild horses do not spend most of their time waiting around in caves (although many predators do). Instead they spend the days and nights traveling around an area of land called the "home range," looking for food. This behavior is called "foraging." It is a combination of feeding and movement. Here are some interesting facts about how horses behave, when they are allowed to:

- In the wild horses spend up to 75% of a 24 hour period eating and moving—*up to 18 hours per day.*
- Because of this a wild herd covers a lot of ground—over 20 miles in an average day. It varies with the seasons and the availability of food, but it could be in excess of 50 miles every day.

So this gives us another bit of information about the horse:

The horse is a traveling animal—a creature of movement

Compare this with the domestic horse that lives in a stable *more* than 18 hours per day, and gets fed "meals" at mealtimes.

Can you see how the way we conventionally keep horses **is in direct opposition** with its natural instincts and needs, and we think like this because of our instincts and needs as predators?

Silent sufferers

Normally, you will never hear a horse crying out in pain or distress in the same way a predator such as a dog will. The reason for this is simple: the horse is a prey animal. A prey animal is "wired" not to tell every predator in the area that it is trapped, in pain, terrified, sick or disabled. This is why horses appear to tolerate the cruelty some human beings inflict on it. This is also why we think it is acceptable to routinely hit horses with sticks and why we can use pain and the threat of pain to drive the horse and make it do our bidding.

- It doesn't mean the horse has no feelings or a high tolerance of pain.

Summary Chapter I: The Truth About Horses

- The horse is a prey animal.
- The horse is a flight animal because it is a prey animal.
- The horse is a herd animal because it is a prey animal.
- The most important emotion a horse has is the need to feel safe.
- The thing that makes horses feel safe is the presence of other animals.
- The horse is a foraging animal.
- The horse is a creature of movement.
- Humans are predators.
- The first thing we do is to prevent the horse from using flight.
- Then we isolate it from the herd, usually in a stable.
- This is in direct conflict with the emotional needs of the horse.

- The horse-human equation is a relationship based on emotional conflict.
- Horses are silent sufferers.

Chapter 2
The Laws of Behavior and Their Consequences

The next "building block" in understanding our relationship with the horse is to understand the forces that work on this relationship. I call these forces *the four laws of behavior*. I call them laws because they are universal, just like the laws of physics, and just like the laws of physics they cannot be bent or broken. They will work all the time, every time, and they are universal because they work on *all* living things, including horses and humans *at the same time*. It also means they will work on *you* whether you believe it or not. After all, you don't have to believe in the law of gravity to fall over.

The laws of behavior are probably most well known and recognizable when they are used in training animals, but actually they are at work all the time. Here is one thing you should understand about them:

- The laws of behavior are incredibly powerful because they work directly with our emotions.

These laws are nothing to do with logical, analytical behavior. They are not rational or a part of free will. That comes afterward. If you think of some examples of common decisions that humans make in their lifetime you will find that *all decisions we make are emotional*, that means they are decided by the emotional laws of behavior, what we then do is *justify them with logic*. Here are some examples:

- the car you drive
- the job you do

- who your partner is
- your political views
- your religious views
- the house you live in
- the clothes you wear
- the food you buy

And finally,

- the horse you ride

All of these are examples of emotional decisions that are then justified with logic, e.g., "I bought this Ferrari because the dealer was offering a really good deal this month." Hmm, well, perhaps not!

If you think this is far-fetched, think about advertising. The billions spent on global advertising every year is spent because the laws of behavior ensure that it will work. Next time you go into the tack shop and come out with something ten minutes before you had no idea existed, yet now you realize you can't live without, you just experienced the laws of behavior in action—again.

So, what are these rules? The best way to understand the rules is to think of them in terms of training a behavior. Whenever we train a behavior we get one of two results, we either cause a behavior to **INCREASE** or we cause a behavior to **DECREASE**.

Let's put this in a table:

INCREASE	DECREASE

- In order to get a behavior to increase we must *reward* it in some way—specifically, we must make it emotionally rewarding.
- The scientific term for emotional reward is **reinforcement**.

A reinforcement is an event that makes a behavior likely to be repeated.

- In order to get a behavior to *decrease* we must make it unpleasant in some way—specifically, we must make it emotionally unpleasant.
- The scientific term for unpleasant emotional experiences is **punishment**.

Whether an event is physically rewarding or punishing is much less important than the emotions it evokes in our minds. For example, imagine you have just run your first marathon but despite your best efforts you just could not finish the race. It was too much for you, and you were forced to drop out. It is very likely that in looking back you will remember every minute of the pain you went through in training, and you will especially remember the humiliation and embarrassment of the moment you decided to drop out. The whole experience becomes a (negative) emotional experience and unless you are an exceptional person it is highly likely that you will never attempt to run another marathon again.

On the other hand, let's say you finished the race. Looking back, you won't remember all the pain and suffering you went through in training, you might not even clearly remember the physical struggle of the race itself, but the thing you *will* remember years later, was the moment of triumph when you finally crossed the line. I call this the "YES!" moment. It is this "yes" moment that is the (positive) emotional reinforcement—and it probably got you thinking about running the next marathon.

Reinforcement

Rewards are also known as *reinforcers* that is, they are actions that are likely to cause a behavior to be repeated and therefore increased. For example, if every time I call my dog to me I give him a piece of meat, he is soon going to be very keen on *increasing* the behavior of coming to me.

If, on the other hand, every time he comes to me I punish him for taking too long or having run off in the first place, he will not want to come toward me and decrease the behavior. In fact he would probably go one step further and actively avoid me or bite me—and I wouldn't blame him. Let's add this to the table:

INCREASE	DECREASE
Reinforce/Reward	Punish

So now we have two types of training and behavior but as there are positives and negatives in everything, so there are positives and negatives in both sides of the table:

INCREASE	DECREASE
Reinforce/Reward	Punish
Positive Reinforcement	**Positive Punishment**
Negative Reinforcement	**Negative Punishment**

This gives us four possible ways of training anything:

- Positive Reinforcement
- Negative Reinforcement
- Positive Punishment
- Negative Punishment

These four possibilities are *the four laws of behavior.* Let's look at each of the laws in greater detail and define them clearly.

Positive Reinforcement

With this law you **add something positive** to the subject's environment. So when I call my dog and reward him with a piece of meat—and thus "positive feelings"—I am using positive reinforcement and the behavior is likely to increase and be repeated.

Negative Reinforcement

With this law you **remove something negative** from the subject's environment but there is a catch here. Usually before you can remove something negative, you have to put it there in the first place. Negative reinforcement is the basis of an incredible amount of human and horse interaction. It is probably the most common way of teaching and learning on the planet. Negative reinforcement can be expressed in many other ways but what it amounts to is **threat**, effectively saying:

- Respond to my wishes or else suffer the consequences!

Which brings us to positive punishment. Positive punishments are *the consequences.*

Positive Punishment

With this law you **add something negative** to the subject's environment like in the second example with my dog in which I punish him if he comes to me. The dog will **decrease** the behavior of coming to me because he doesn't like it! We are now on the *decreasing* side of the table. After a very few repetitions my unfortunate dog will learn not to come to me at all because of the *threat* of being punished. So he is responding to fear of the emotional threat not the actual punishment.

Negative Punishment

With this law you must **remove something positive** from the animal's environment. Once again the positive thing being removed is something perceived as emotionally positive. Usually this is a **freedom** to behave in a desired way. For example, if you decide to keep your horse in isolation in a stable and away from other horses, you are removing the animal's basic freedom and need to be in the safety of the herd—all forms of negative punishment. Negative punishment is often associated with the animal's environment in some way.

This gives us the four possible ways of training a horse.

Summary of the laws of behavior

INCREASE	DECREASE
Reinforce/Reward	Punish
Positive Reinforcement	**Positive Punishment**
Add something positive	Add something negative
Negative Reinforcement	**Negative Punishment**
Remove something negative	Remove something positive

The coercion test

I mentioned just now that it was possible to use negative punishment (remove something positive) and positive punishment (add something negative) as a threat in the form of:

"Comply with my wishes or else suffer the consequences."

I call the statement above the coercion test. It is a way of understanding whether you are using negative reinforcement and the threat of positive punishment on your horse. If you are ever saying to your horse, "comply with my wishes..." then you are acting coercively. Negative reinforcement and positive punishment always work together like this. The first point to make is:

- Despite being a form of coercion, negative reinforcement is not always a "bad" thing.

This is because there is an element of choice for the horse. Of course, it may not always be a very good choice, but the horse can engage its natural defenses as a *temporary* measure while under this pressure. But the little word "or" means that the horse can choose to avoid "the consequences." This is why it is used in training horses. The horse, in a limited way, can choose to do the right thing. But...

- Negative reinforcement is also not always a "good" thing.

If we ask the horse to make a choice and we apply a sanction if the horse makes the wrong choice (a correction), we are essentially using a **threat**. This makes the horse choose between something it wants to do and something it has to do. If we force this choice, we are using *coercion*. Understanding coercion and its consequences is another of those important things you must learn about horses.

Here is a dictionary definition of what coercion really means:

Coercion is the practice of compelling an individual to involuntarily behave in a certain way (whether through action or inaction) by use of threats, intimidation or some other form of pressure or force. Coercion may typically involve the actual infliction of physical or psychological harm in order to enhance the credibility of a threat. The threat of further harm may then lead to the cooperation or obedience of the person being coerced. The term is often associated with circumstances which involve the unethical use of threats or harm to achieve some objective.

Horses and threats

Horses have to deal with threats as a part of their natural lives. Threats can come not just from predators but from the environment. For example, drought, starvation, flood, extreme cold or extreme heat are common environmental threats. Threats can also come from other horses or herbivores in the form of competition. Even disease or parasites are a threat to the life of a horse, but horses are naturally able to deal with all these things because there is usually an element of choice that will defer the threat. Horses attempt to defer threats in one of three ways. You might be able to guess the first two as they are well known. They are **flight** or **fight**.

Flight

Avoidance is obviously the first reaction of a flight animal. Flight animals are built to run away, everything about their physical body tells us this. The large nostrils to suck in air, the explosive power in their back ends, the giant lungs that fill two-thirds of the body cavity, and the super efficient arrangement of legs, each traveling on one efficient toe. They are superbly adapted to do this for physical flight. Flight, however, can also be a mental thing as we will see in a moment.

The second reaction to threat—*usually when flight is not an option*—is fight.

Fight

Fight is also fairly obvious when it is physical. Horses may be gentle herbivores but they are certainly not defenseless.

- Have you ever seen a horse that destroyed its stable from the inside out? Here the option of flight was taken away, so the horse lashed out (literally) at the surrounding threat.

- Have you ever seen a horse and rider fight their way around a show jumping ring? What is taken away? Once again, escape or flight.

Fight, like flight can also be a mental thing. For example, horses can turn aggressively on other horses or human beings and *sometimes even on themselves*. Self-harming is very disturbing to see but fortunately not that common. I have seen it and it is important to remember it is a *reaction*, not a cause. The horse wasn't born this way and it's not its fault. *The cause is always a threat from which the horse cannot escape through flight.* Talking of things that cannot be escaped, the third reaction to threat or coercion is an extension of the flight reaction—the mental flight reaction—that I call "compliance."

Compliance

Horses are survivors. They will do what they can to remain alive. They are also intelligent so they will work out what is the *least* dangerous, stressful or painful way to avoid the coercive thing. The key word in that sentence is "least," because compliance is always typified by the phrase **"minimal effort."**

After all, they have no incentive to do anything more.

Minimal effort

The problem of minimal effort is a major drawback for trainers who use these methods. In a later section of this book, I will look at some of the systems that are based on negative reinforcement including both conventional systems and last century's natural horsemanship techniques, based on concepts such as:

- increasing pressure
- pressure and release
- approach and retreat
- habituation
- yielding to pressure and so on

All of these techniques are founded on the idea of, "do what I want or else suffer the consequences."

Very few of these systems actually get to the stage of inflicting actual pain or "cruelty" on the animal because they appear to work so effectively as threats. But the truth is, these methods are highly inefficient because the horse is only making the minimal effort—just enough to defer the coercive stimulus. The popular notion of yielding to pressure is an example of this. Horses that appear to be yielding to pressure are actually just evading pressure. What is in it for the horse is the removal of the coercive stimulus. It has nothing to do with a wish to please the human or to "obey."

A horse that is truly yielding to pressure is one that is looking for a positive emotional reward or is actively trying to do the "right" thing because it knows that the "right" answer will lead to good emotions. This is the opposite of minimal effort—*maximum effort*. I'll go more into the topic of communication- and trust-based training and the benefits resulting from this type of training in Chapter 11.

More compliance

Probably the clearest examples of compliant horses are those in riding stables that are made to perform the same actions day after day. They are the horses that take people for their first ride or take them on a "pony ride" around the same paths over and over again. Sadly these horses are virtual robots, switched off from their surroundings as if accepting their fate. Unlike other horses they are no longer tuned in to what is going on around them. They take no notice of sights, sounds and smells as they make a totally minimal effort. But, as we now know, horses are prey animals. Imagine the implications of this behavior to a prey animal! These are horses that feel they no longer have the option of their natural defenses of flight and fight. All that remains for them is compliance. The most serious implication of compliance is not its effect on the horse, it is its effect on the human.

- Most humans are rewarded by this behavior because they misinterpret compliance as **obedience**. It is not.

Compliance is a last resort for the horse. The horse can never win because the coercion never goes away—it just becomes tolerable. Yet at the same time it *prolongs* the total coercive experience indefinitely. As we will see in later chapters there are internal mental and physical reactions to this state and they are not good news for the horse. This form of mental flight may go on for years, which is why negative reinforcement is a very inefficient (and not especially ethical) way to train horses. Minimal effort is why it takes some horses years of their life to master even elementary training in a discipline such as dressage.

I said that even compliance has a small element of choice about it, and in that sense can be seen as a "good" thing, but what happens when humans put horses in situations from which they can never escape? Situations in which, flight, fight and even compliance are not an option? Usually when this situation is encountered by the horse, it is connected with more than just a coercive stimulus that might be avoided. It is connected to a scenario in which *the whole environment* is the coercive threat.

Stress

When the horse's environment becomes one of unavoidable coercion, we have a name for it: stress. Here are some examples of environmental coercion:

- horses that live for prolonged periods in stables
- horses that are blanketed for many months, if not throughout the year
- horses that are fed what their owner believes is "good" for them
- horses that wear horseshoes
- horses that are shaved of their natural coat
- horses that live in isolation from other horses
- horses that are unable to travel or escape
- horses that are unable to feed on what they want, when they want
- horses that are drugged

And many other scenarios, unfortunately also including the activity we call riding. In all of these situations the horse has no choice, which means that the horse is always in an environment that is forced upon it.

Enforcement is the opposite of choice; and enforcement is the opposite of freedom; enforcement is also the deliberate and methodical application of stress.

I will return to this subject in later sections of the book but for the present it might be worthwhile considering the list above in light of what we learned in the last chapter, i.e., the horse is a herd animal, a flight animal and a foraging animal. You will notice that in each case the enforced environment conflicts with the natural needs of the horse and usually provides the exact opposite.

It might be interesting to consider when the enforced state might be part of the natural life of the horse. Flight and fight are strategies that have an element of choice but extreme mental compliance is the only possible reaction to a threat that is unavoidable. The time that a horse would experience this in a natural situation is in the last few moments of their lives, when they are trapped by a predator or in the final stages of disease. The horse becomes helpless, or put another way the horse gives itself up to its fate. Horses that do this are still attempting to escape by flight but the physical option is no longer there, so mental flight is all that is left.

I think you can see that not only is coercion—in any form—not a particularly nice thing to inflict on a horse, but that is not the main reason you must avoid it. You must avoid it because coercion works both ways, by which I mean, **coercion has fallout**.

Laws of coercion

The best ways of learning about this fallout—or more accurately the side effects of coercion—is to see it in terms of what I call the laws of coercion. Once again these are universal laws. They are not limited to horses as they apply to all species, all the time, including us. The variations on these laws are many and subtle, but here are the three most common ones:

- Coercion is positively reinforcing for the coercer.
- Coercion always generates more coercion.
- Coercion always generates avoidance or violence also known as counter coercion.

Coercion is always positively reinforcing for the coercer

Horses are prey animals while human instincts and much of our behavior is based on our background as predators. One example of this, no matter how we dress it up and intellectualize it, is how we find the coercion of prey animals hugely rewarding.

Note: This doesn't make us "bad" people, it just means we are using the instincts we inherited from our ancestors—instincts that helped them survive and instincts that are partly responsible for our present existence. It is exactly the same for the horse. It is using all the instincts and behaviors that have helped it to survive for millions of years by opposing the will of predators. If we can understand this and accept it, then we will make a huge leap forward in our understanding of our horse **and of ourselves**.

Of course, we don't chase, capture, kill and eat horses very much nowadays but we certainly use some variation of those activities when we train them. We still chase and capture them almost every day of their lives.

- A lot of human behavior that has grown up around domestic horses in the last few thousand years is based on **our hunting instincts**.

I believe this is why so many humans behave like predators when they are around prey animals—not because they are "bad" people but because it feels *instinctively* right to do these things and we are *positively rewarded* by emotions like satisfaction, a sense of accomplishment, a sense of control, a feeling of superiority and so on.

And this begs the question:

Do horses use coercion?

Absolutely! I'm sure you have seen a horse flatten its ears and threaten to lunge at or bite another horse. This is coercion in the form of negative reinforcement and it is therefore reinforcing for the horse to get its way and move the other horse. This is also an example of negative punishment used in a "good" way by allowing the choice of flight or fight. The horse that is being moved may not be happy about it but it can always move out of the way (usually using minimal effort) and thus can in some way "control" the coercive stimulus of the other horse.

- People and horses use coercion because it is a way of getting what you want and getting good feelings about it!

That is coercive side effect number one: *coercion is always positively reinforcing for the coercer.* Because it is positively reinforcing for the coercer we are on the increasing side of the table. Coercive side effect number two is:

Coercion always generates more coercion

Have you ever seen someone get on a horse and kick it to go? What did they do when the horse didn't go? They kicked it again—harder. Coercion is ultimately a downward spiral for the coerced. What advice do some people give you about a horse that is already in a strong bit? Get a stronger one. If our threat of coercion does not work, we always increase the threat level, either by

- increasing its intensity
- increasing its frequency
- trying a different form of coercion

So you might ask, if the first law of coercion is always positively reinforcing for the coercer and the second law says coercion must always increase is there ever an end result to this downward spiral? Is there ever a way a horse can escape it? We have seen how the state of compliance is one reaction to unavoidable coercion, and compliance is a form of mental flight, but there is one more reaction to coercion: *fight*, both mental and physical. The technical name for this is *counter coercion*. This brings us to the third law of coercion:

Coercion generates counter coercion

Coercion is a negative thing and negative things, especially *emotions* and *experiences* are cumulative, which means they attract more negatives. Eventually these negatives generate *avoidance* or *violence* in the form of counter coercion, in other words:

- The coerced will attempt to turn on the the coercer.

Violence is also called fight and, is frequently accompanied by flight (avoidance). It is really important to fully understand these reactions if you want to get good with horses.

From the predator point of view, flight and fight are very inconvenient and frustrating reactions and *that is exactly what they are supposed to be.* To a horse, however, they are vital tools in their armory. They are the emergency defense mechanisms needed to survive and oppose the will of predators. Consequently horses are very good at using them. Counter coercion is how horses resist our will.

Here are some examples:

- Have you ever desperately held onto or parted company with a horse that has been trying to avoid your coercion through flight? This is what happens when horses "explode" or bolt.
- Have you ever been kicked or bitten or barged? This is fight.
- Have you been on a horse that reared? This is fight also.

One way to look at this, and many people do this, is to see the horse's behavior as "deliberate disobedience" and even "bad manners." They think the horse is intentionally trying to do the opposite of what they want and this would be very reasonable *if the horse were another human being* but it is not. It is a horse and it is doing what prey animals have been programmed to do for millions of years. We can't blame them for this, they are following their instincts, just as we are.

Later in the book I will look at this strange idea that humans have of interpreting horse behavior as human behavior, but for now just accept these behaviors as counter coercion and a perfectly natural reaction to being coerced by a predator.

Counter coercion is the most powerful *and dangerous* reaction to coercion. Don't become a victim of it. The only way to avoid it altogether is *not to use coercion at all!* All real horse people—horse-whisperers—know this, and that is why they don't use coercive training methods. Not because they don't work, *they do;* but because the disadvantages of the laws of coercion *do not make them effective ways of training horses.*

The laws of behavior and us

In case you think the laws of behavior are something that only affect our horses, let me give you some examples of how these laws affect humans and their cultures:

- The legal system is based on negative reinforcement and the threat of positive punishment. Governments say "comply with our laws or else suffer the consequences."

- The commercial world and especially advertising, is based on promises of positive reinforcement and the benefits of a product. Any salesman will tell you we never buy "things," we buy "good feelings."

- Most religions, and I don't mean any one in particular, are based on a principle called self-denial. In other words, "behave in a certain way today and you will reap a reward in the future or possibly even a future life."

- Our education system is based around negative reinforcement and positive punishment. For example, exams are an effective threat strategy, "work hard and pass the exams or else fail the course."

- In fact, every aspect of human behavior and every interaction we have with our fellow human is based in some way on the laws of behavior.

Coercion and culture

Just as behavioral laws influence us, so does our reaction to them. Three of the laws of behavior are essentially coercive in nature so they generate coercive reactions and obey the laws of coercion.

- Terrorism is counter coercion and fight.
- Refugees and political asylum seekers are in a state of flight from a coercive environment.
- Crime is fight.
- Gambling is based on negative punishment and the expectation of positive reinforcement.
- Health, wealth, happiness, and freedom are values all based on positive reinforcement.

In the next chapter I will begin to look at how we care for horses, how we train them and how we manage them or, as I suggested in Chapter 1—how we *think* about them. But before that, here is a summary of this chapter:

Summary Chapter 2: The Laws of Behavior and Their Consequences

There are four possible laws:

- Positive reinforcement: Add something positive
- Negative reinforcement: Remove something negative
- Positive punishment: Add something negative
- Negative punishment: Remove something positive

Negative reinforcement and positive punishment work together in the form of threats and the test for this is to ask are you saying, "comply with my wishes or else suffer the consequences."

Negative reinforcement, positive punishment and negative punishment are all types of coercion.

There are three reactions to coercion:

- Flight (avoidance)

- Fight (violence)
- Compliance (always a state in which the subject makes *minimal effort*)

There are three major side-effects of coercion and they are called *the laws of coercion*:

- Coercion is always positively reinforcing for the coercer.
- Coercion always generates more coercion. Coercion will always increase either in intensity, frequency or type.
- Coercion always generates counter coercion, usually avoidance or violence.

The laws of behavior affect every aspect of our culture and interaction with other human beings and animals.

Chapter 3
The Four Models of Horsemanship

The way we think about our horses is probably the single biggest day-to-day influence on our animals. It may not mean much to us, and indeed, we may never have thought of this as being important before, but your horses know exactly how you think about them, because they have to deal with the consequences of your thinking every day of their lives.

To begin with, we need a way of understanding the whole complex world of interaction between our two species and to do this I introduce the concept of a model.

- A model is a collection of ideas that represent reality. For example, an architect's model is a physical model built from a plan originating in the architect's imagination. The model allows others to visualize what the finished building will look like in terms of shape, color and setting, etc., without getting lost in details like door hinges or plumbing.

There are many models of human behavior, belief and understanding, but for now, the one we are interested in is a model that represents the relationship between our two species. This is a mental model of all the things we do with our horse, for example:

- how we feed it
- how we house it
- how we treat it if it is sick

- how we train it

- how we breed it

- and so on...

So a model is all the things we do to our horses, but it is much more than this. All of us create these mental models in our minds, and everyone has a slightly different model. We sometimes describe this as our "belief system." Consequently all of us hold different beliefs based on our experiences. This is how our brains make sense of all the information taken in by our senses. If we could not do this we would be overwhelmed by being alive. So a model represents all the things humans *think* about horses or more accurately, all the things humans *believe* about horses.

In the next few chapters I will explain four possible models of thinking about horses—all very different from each other. They represent the four ways humans think about horses and therefore, *four ways that horses experience humans*. This is important because some situations created by humans make horses completely dependent on the beliefs of their human owners for their daily existence. In the later models we will see that it doesn't have to be like this, but for now, let's take a look at a good example of this type of thinking—the utility model.

The Utility Model

The utility model is based on *tradition*—the traditions of culture and history. There are many different variations of the utility model but they all come from tried and tested knowledge about *what works and what doesn't*. This is this model's greatest strength as well as its greatest weakness. After all, if something has worked perfectly for hundreds of years, why bother to change it? The problem is that once we have found out what works, we are reluctant to try other options that might work even better, so we find ourselves applying the same logic of 150 years ago. In this way traditional thinking can trace its roots way back into history. To understand this more deeply, imagine yourself back about 150 years. In the UK this puts you back in the time of The British Empire and Queen Victoria. Consider the relationship between horses and humans at that time.

Very few horses were owned simply for *leisure and pleasure* as there are today. In fact, almost all horses were owned *for a reason*. They had a use—a function—or as I put it, they had a *utility*. For example, if the horse was a large, strong, draft type then it probably pulled a plow or a wagon. If it was a certain breed or size or color it might have a career in the army. Other horses were used to pull carriages or to carry service providers such as the local doctor on his rounds. In fact it was the horse's utility that *defined the animal, including its value*. It affected all those things I described in the model above: diet, breeding, training, etc. It is important to realize that the human was also utterly dependent on the horse's ability to do its job. Quite literally, in some cases, the life and livelihood of the human depended on the horse's utility.

If we look at our modern English riding we can still see the influence of the utility model everywhere, because it is still very much with us. Even today, many horses are defined by their use. Any horse that can be described as a working or sport horse lives within the utility model. If a horse is a police horse or an army horse, it is within the utility model. In the world of sport, a polo pony or a racehorse, an eventing horse, a dressage horse, a show jumper and so on—all of these are examples of the utility horse.

If you think about your own case and those of your horse-owning friends, do you think of your horses as having a basic purpose? Even if your horse is "only" a riding horse or does a few local shows and is basically owned for leisure and pleasure, (most horses nowadays are owned for these reasons), do you still think of the activities you do with your horse as important because that is what your horse **is for**? If you do, then this is your utility model.

- Have you ever noticed when you meet people and they find out that you own a horse, the first question they ask is "what do you DO with your horse?" Most people believe horses need to have a function.

In English riding one particular set of traditions had a much greater influence than any other—the *cavalry* utility model. Today many of the habits and customs associated with English riding are traceable back to the British army of 150 years ago. For instance, it is the habit of almost all English riders to mount their horses on the left side of the horse. This is a tradition that is passed down through the generations and is taught to almost all novice riders. But where does this idea come from? Originally this became standardized so that the cavalry sword, worn on the left side of the trooper, did not get in the way as he mounted. Not many riders today carry a sword, yet we still religiously climb up on the left side a hundred years after it was no longer necessary. This is a great illustration of the pervasive power of tradition.

One particular period of history that had enormous influence was the time of the British Raj in India. Today almost all English riders wear jodhpurs, a particular type of riding trousers invented in the city of Jodhpur in India. Many people attend gymkhanas, a descendent of the inter-regimental competitions held between cavalry units. Gymkhana is a word that comes from the Hindi language. The English equivalent of the American "saddle cloth" is called a numnah, a word that comes from the Urdu language.

The influence of cavalry from the 19th and 20th century permeates almost every aspect of life in a traditional English stable yard. Here just some of the many examples:

- the daily routine of keeping horses in stalls, and all it entails
- the strict adherence to feeding times and the concept of "meals"
- the English obsession with the appearance and grooming of their horses
- geometric patterns around the school during lessons
- group behaviors and drills in lessons
- instructors and "recruits"
- uniforms, boots and helmets
- posture and appearance—a good seat
- the importance of correct training, usually based on the idea of "correction"
- obsessive interest in the "right" way of doing things
- fondness for discipline and application of the rules
- appearance of the "yard"
- and so on...

Its influence is especially strong in the training programs we use on our horses, for example:

- *Lunging or longeing* (UK and American spellings) was a military training exercise used to get a raw recruit and a raw horse together in the most practical and efficient way.

- The *equipment* we put on our horses, especially the traditional *English saddle* is primarily developed from the light flexible saddles used by the cavalry.

- This design is now the main saddle type used in most equestrian sports all of which began as military competitions or activities.

English riders typically wear a *uniform*, usually consisting of long or short jodhpur boots, jodhpurs or breeches, sometimes a jacket such as a show jacket or less formal hacking jacket, depending on the occasion and *always* a riding helmet. This last one is unusual as it is not a legal requirement to wear a helmet in the UK, (although it may be perfectly sensible to wear one). This is primarily a cultural tradition as other riding styles in other countries do not consider the wearing of a helmet as either necessary or practical, although this is changing for safety reasons outside of tradition.

Control

The riding style of English riders is based around control of the horse's natural behavior by use of reins and a bit, and the concept of the *correct seat. Control over our horse's behavior is an important military idea.* It is also the root of many people's ideas about *dominance* and *discipline*, both concepts rigorously applied in the training of horses and riders. In English riding it is usual to ride with *contact* maintained with the horse's mouth through the use of the bridle and bit (see section on the utility model and other cultures, below).

In the Victorian cavalry, control took the form of unquestioning *obedience* of both horse and rider to a perceived standard of behavior. This legacy still pervades many equestrian sports such as dressage, where a judgment is made on how a horse and rider compare against a perfect ideal of performance. The greater the level of control, the greater the performance. The precise nature of turns, gaits and geometric patterns in the dressage arena further emphasizes the parade-ground heritage of the dressage discipline.

Uniforms and uniformity

One particularly persistent legacy of the cavalry utility model is the idea of *uniformity* or *conformity*. This is pure military thinking and a descendent of the idea of unquestioning obedience in both horse and rider. When conformity is combined with the inherent rigidity of the utility model, the result is predictably that new ideas take a long time to filter through, but when they do, they are readily adopted by all (ironically, with exactly the same absolute loyalty that people showed to the previous "unbreakable rules").

Another military legacy is the idea of "mirrored behaviors." You will often see examples of this in the equestrian world with fellow riders who adopt the same clothing and tack—even the same type and color of horse—immaculately turned out and mirroring each others movements. This is especially true of riders in group lessons attempting to create perfect geometric patterns in the sand—each horse moving in impeccable sequence with all the others—as they imitate the parade grounds of the British Raj in India 150 years ago.

The Utility Model and other cultures

The other main global "style" of riding is the *western* style. Although this riding technique has completely different roots to its English counterpart, and it promotes very different ideas of the right or wrong way to do things, it was still developed as part of a utility model. The saddle and bridle are very different to that of English riding, descending from the Arabic and Spanish cultures and eventually adapted by the needs and traditions of the US cattle industry. A saddle was needed that could be used for long periods during the work day and which allowed equipment to be carried and ropes attached. Along with this, a riding style arose that allowed the rider free use of his hands for other tasks. Consequently western riders use much less rein contact and give guidance to the horse through shifts in weight. This is reflected in western equestrian sports many of which are based on things like maneuverability and speed. The gallop, spin turns and sliding stops are an important part of western sports such as reining, yet these abilities (that all horses have), are rarely, if ever, used in English riding. It is useful to note that the western utility model is also the main influence of many of the "natural horsemanship" systems used today.

Although the English and western cultures are very different, **both** can be considered as being developed for practical purposes within different utility models. Both represent a clear and simple relationship and both are based on what works and what doesn't work as well as what is practical and efficient.

There are several other influences to the English utility model, for example, the French influence found especially within the dressage world. Words like, piaffe (lit: to stamp, or paw the ground) passage, puissance (power), and of course dressage (schooling) and many others. Dressage also developed originally from a military utility model.

The Utility Model and tools

Utility models often use mechanical devices to modify or inhibit a horse's natural behavior. You might think it is fairly obvious that natural behavior such as running away in a state of panic from anything the horse is afraid of is a potentially dangerous behavior and it would be sensible to want to control it. Therefore, humans would be completely justified in suppressing it, but the situation is more complex than that. Every behavior shown by a horse in a utility model context is defined by the horse's purpose, *therefore*:

- The natural behavior of the horse **has no place** because it is not related to the horse's function.

Over the centuries many devices such as bits, bridles, training aids and techniques, whips, spurs etc., have been developed by humans to control unwanted, but nevertheless perfectly natural behavior in the horse.

Note: Training aids and training techniques have **not** (usually) been developed with the aim of being deliberately cruel to the horse, for that would not fit with the horse's function, but simply with the goal of having the horse behave in a way that was practical and efficient and that caused it to be able to fulfill its purpose or utility.

Practical and efficient

Practical and *efficient* as you may have noticed, are two words used a lot within with the utility model. Practical and efficient usually means:

- practical and efficient in terms of time
- practical and efficient in terms of effort
- practical and efficient in terms of money

The Utility Model and professionals

The ideas of the utility model are not just associated with horses and their riders. Professionals, such as vets, farriers, equine dentists, horse trainers and so on, are all working within their own utility model. They have knowledge, skills and traditions that have developed to achieve the objectives of their profession in the most practical and efficient, tried and tested way. This is not a bad thing, they will know what works and what doesn't, and it is for this knowledge that we pay them. However, something I have learned about professionals over the years, is that they tend to see problems in terms of the tools they have to solve the issues they are called to address. The upshot of this is that a vet, for example, will invariably see a problem in terms of drugs or surgery, a farrier will often view the same problem as a shoeing issue, an equine dentist will suggest a problem with teeth and so on. In other words, if your tools consist of a set of hammers, everything begins to look like a type of nail.

This **does not** mean that the advice you are given and the treatment your horse gets is not valid, but be aware that professionals are still human beings with an understandable human tendency to look at a situation from their own perspective and intuition, and also to base their diagnosis on the tools, knowledge and training with which they're most familiar.

Veterinary knowledge comes from the traditional utility model of the profession, and certainly in the case of equine vets a great deal of this knowledge was originally based on experience learned from treating traumatic injuries to horses on the battlefield. It is interesting to note that even in the medical profession a lot of the modern surgical skills with human trauma injuries date back to the need to treat battlefield casualties.

Here is an example of this type of thinking. Take for instance, a fictitious vet presented with a case of laminitis. Initially, the short-term diagnosis will be based around (quite rightly) pain-relief and further prevention.

Note: Laminitis is a painful condition that causes chronic lameness in horses due to a swelling if the laminae or membranes within the hoof. Also known as founder.

But from a larger perspective, laminitis is actually an *environmental* issue. Recent research points toward many possible causes behind laminitis. Here are a few:

- abnormalities in the modern diet that we feed our horses

- a lack of movement

- the wearing of horseshoes

- the type of grasses that are available

- the effect of long term stress

- complex disorders such as Cushing's disease

When a vet sees a laminitic case they will typically suggest that the horse is first isolated in a stable or restricted area then put on a "diet" restricting its food intake in some way. When we deal with the second model of horsemanship, you will come to understand why this type of diagnosis is made and how, in all probability, *it will compile the problem and make things **worse** for the horse.* This is truly a utility model "bandage" solution.

Bandage solutions

Although the true causes of a situation may be complex and varied, one of the major drawbacks of the utility model—as in the case of the laminitic horse or pony—is its single solution approach. This single solution will appear most *practical and efficient* and will, often, even appear to work, but it obscures the complex nature of multiple actual causes. I call this type of thinking "*bandage mentality*" because it is a very human tendency to choose the easy, short-term solution—*obscuring the truth of the situation.* Another problem with bandage solutions is that often they are based on superstition.

Superstition

Many of the ideas that have grown up surrounding the utility model are based on beliefs that are superstitious in nature:

- Superstition is the belief in things that are emotionally satisfying but factually wrong.

Every utility model of horse keeping in the world has hundreds or even thousands of superstition-based rules and beliefs about the right and wrong ways of doing things. This fits perfectly with the military mindset before it. However, you might be surprised to learn this *sometimes* extends to professional advice as well.

Continuing the example of a laminitic pony above, the vet prescribes stall rest and a restricted diet. This is interesting because we should ask ourselves what **every** human being on the planet does when they feel unwell, regardless of culture or race? They retire to their "inner-sanctum" or **bed**, a place where they feel safe, protected and can begin the healing process.

Now let's consider how many horses in the history of horses have voluntarily and deliberately isolated themselves from the herd when they are unwell? Answer: not a single solitary one—ever.

In other words, our vet is not basing his treatment on horse behavior at all. He is basing it on his own human feelings because it is emotionally satisfying to do so. This is superstition.

A further superstitious event here is placing the horse on a "diet" to restrict its food intake. But as we have seen, a horse is a fiber-digesting animal that has evolved to trickle feed for up to 18 hours per day. Its prey animal digestive system is not designed to experience periods of fasting, but predator digestive systems like ours are designed to do exactly that. Attempting to switch the digestive system on and off like this can be very dangerous for a horse and may make its situation worse. The reality is that the causes of conditions such as laminitis are many and complex, and are not likely to be treated with superficial "bandage solutions."

Once again, I would like to make it *really clear*, this is not a "bad" vet—just a very human one. Vets, like the rest of us, are driven by our human emotions—something I witnessed growing up with a veterinarian father.

Superstition is everywhere in the horse world and it constantly reinforces our human emotions. Especially in the utility model, it is the main reason why inaccurate beliefs are passed down through generations.

The Utility Model and the media

The media love the utility model, especially in the form of offering advice from an *expert*. There is something comforting in being able to relax and accept what we are told without worrying about it. We tend to accept as truth whatever experts suggest based on their utility models *but have you ever noticed how you can always find an expert that will tell you the exact opposite?*

The media gives false authority to the opinions of experts and this authority perpetuates the validity of these views. In fact, when one expert contradicts another it is frequently little more than a conflict of different sets of superstitious beliefs. Given the example above perhaps you can see why that might be.

This is the basic process by which, over the years, the ideas of various authorities become traditional wisdom and sometimes urban myth; this is how things become accepted as the "right" way to do things; this is how rules, regulations, traditions, and superstitions have come to dominate the utility model—and this is why we still climb on our horses from the left side.

The Utility Model is a masculine model

There are two interesting points to be made about this model. First, it is primarily a *masculine* model developed by men, for men. The proportion of women to men involved in the horse world 150 years ago was the opposite of what we know today. Even where men are involved with horses today, relatively few are purely leisure and pleasure riders. Most work in the utility model as professional riders, trainers, breeders, etc., pursuing a career with horses to earn a living. If you look at the equestrian professions of vets, farriers, stud farm owners and carriers, etc., traditionally these, too, have been male, although this is changing rapidly. Certainly 20 or 30 years ago, the utility model was almost exclusively male.

The Utility Model and money

Next, the utility model is often associated with **generating** *money*. This is when the words "practical" and "efficient" are applied most rigorously. Whether it is prize money in a competition or breeding horses or trading horses usually there is a financial aspect to the utility model associated with business. This is reflected in the value of utility model horses. Horses at the top of the utility model can be worth millions, however there is one very important issue here, **the value of a utility horse is solely dependent on its function.** If the animal can no longer fulfill that function, for whatever reason, its value can drop to zero *in an instant!* The world is awash with formerly valuable horses, now free to good homes.

One of my own horses is a good example of this idea that a horse's value is linked to its function. This horse was an army eventing horse, advertised one year for just under £10,000, yet the following year—after an accident and insurance claim—he was given away for nothing.

The Utility Model has a high fallout rate

To illustrate this more clearly, let's return to thinking about how we regard a dog or cat compared with a horse. As I've mentioned, very few people would consider selling the family cat or dog, yet horses are bought and sold and "disposed of" every day. Why is this?

It is because they are perceived by humans as **needing** to have a purpose and that purpose is linked to their monetary value.

Some people argue that a horse must have a purpose simply to rationalize the expense. When a horse without a use is viewed by the very industry built around it as a "useless expense," the lives of horses become not just undervalued, but "disposable." This is why once-pampered horses end up in feedlots with one final, remote chance of being found by rescue organizations before they are killed.

We attribute a high emotional (sentimental) value to dogs, yet, outside of a working utility model, we would not normally asses their value in terms of money. However with horses we do exactly the opposite, they may have a high perceived monetary value based on purpose, but are assigned a non-emotional (unsentimental) value and so may be "traded" when they no longer suit our purposes and ambitions.

Utility Model limitations

The biggest limitation of the utility model is its rigidity when anything unassociated with the horse's function is considered irrelevant. If understanding the horse as a wild animal is viewed as irrelevant to improving its specific function, the treatment of horses is further limited to traditional approaches and solutions of 150 years ago, including those based on superstition.

Another problem with the utility model is its connection with money. If a human invests a great deal of hard-earned cash in a horse then it might be reasonable to argue the horse must fulfill the function for which it was purchased. This idea relates back to historical times when horses filled the role now mostly taken by machines. This argument is very powerful yet it begs the question of whether it is morally or ethically right to regard animals as machines or commodities. Most people would say it isn't, but they aren't the ones paying the money.

Finally it is worth asking the question, "How much influence does the horse have in how it is treated within the utility model? The answer is, of course, **none**.

This is the utility model, in a moment we will turn to the second model which I call the anthropomorphic model, but first a summary of the utility model:

Summary of Chapter 3: The Utility Model

- A horse is defined solely by its use; anything outside of this definition is irrelevant unless it enhances the horses function.

- The utility model is a simple, clear (unsentimental) and practical relationship.

- The utility model is based on historical traditions.

- In English riding these traditions are primarily from the cavalry model of the late 1800s.

- The western utility model is based on the Arabic and Spanish models and the American cattle industry.

- There are many utility models, for example veterinary or agricultural.

- They are based on what is believed to be tried and tested and what is practical and efficient.

- This leads to bandage solutions that solve problems in the most practical and efficient, short-term way.

- Bandage solutions, mindless beliefs, rules and regulations are variations on one thing, superstition.

- Superstitions are beliefs that are emotionally satisfying but factually wrong.

- The utility model is enthusiastically promoted through the media by "experts."

- An expert can always be found to contradict another expert.

- The utility model is a model created largely by men, for men.

- The utility model is frequently associated with the acquisition of money.

- The utility model is rigid and difficult to change.

- The horse has no influence in the utility model.

- The utility model has a high fall-out rate.
- Horses are regarded as having high monetary value but low emotional/sentimental value.
- Dogs and cats, etc., are the opposite.

Chapter 4
The Anthropomorphic Model

This section deals with a model of horsemanship called the anthropomorphic model.

- Understanding this model will give you a **major insight** into the relationship between horses and humans.

Understanding anthropomorphism and its consequences will change forever the way you look at horses and other animals. You will realize why there are so many problems with the health of horses as well as our relationships to them, and you will understand why a lot of the things we want to do with our horses actually put us in direct confrontation with them. Understanding anthropomorphism will also help you see why so much of our relationship is obscured by *confusion*—for both us and our horses—because most of our anthropomorphic ideas are based on warm, affectionate feelings towards our horses yet their impact leads to fear, coercion, danger, injury and even long term sickness and premature death.

Here is a bold statement. Please try to let it sink in, but above all, stick with me through the rest of this chapter **no matter how much you think you disagree with me.** I *promise* it will make more sense by the end:

Anthropomorphism is the single biggest threat to the health and well-being of horses *and their riders* in the world today, despite the fact that it is based on human notions of benevolence and kindness.

So how did all this start?

Up until the end of WWII, the utility model formed the basis of almost all the relationships between horses and human beings. It was after the war that things began to change for the horse. Machines started to take the place of functions formerly performed by the horse, and horses without a function started to be seen as an expensive luxury. Fortunately, as leisure time and disposable income increased, more and more people considered owning horses for leisure and pleasure purposes. Along with this change in people's circumstances, their attitudes began to soften. I believe this was largely due to a rather strange phenomenon that is unique to the horse world. Men, who for centuries had completely dominated the horse world, began to drift away in pursuit of machines such as cars and motorbikes, and this led to an increasing involvement of women with horses. To an "outsider" this change of gender dominance must appear quite remarkable. Official figures in the UK put the ratio of female to male involvement in the equestrian world as 75% female to 25% male. However, if you remove the number of men who are involved with horses in a purely utility model capacity (breeders, trainers, etc.) and count only those men who own horses purely for leisure and pleasure, I believe the ratio is much, much higher in favor of women. This is even more remarkable when you consider 100 years ago the situation was completely reversed.

I mentioned in Chapter 1 that one thing that most defines your relationship with the horse is what you believe about him. We will see that in two of the models men and women tend to have very different beliefs about horses. This change in the eyes of a horse must be deeply profound. Following the second world war, the purely practical, almost mechanical mindset of the utility model became replaced by one of *benevolence and kind feelings* toward our faithful friend. Although humans continued to use the methods of the existing utility model, they adapted them into the system we know today: the *anthropomorphic model of horsemanship*. It is now the most popular model of horsemanship in the world.

So what is anthropomorphism?

A dictionary will define anthropomorphism something like this:

The attribution of human motivation, characteristics, or behavior to inanimate objects, animals, or natural phenomena.

At its simplest level, it is about interpreting the behavior of animals in human terms.

I always know when I am dealing with anthropomorphic owners because they often describe what their horse is "thinking." They will have elaborate explanations for their horses' behavior without taking into consideration any of the natural and basic motivations of horses as prey animals (as discussed in Chapter 1). Although these explanations are emotionally rewarding and supportive of the relationships they most want, they leave out simple facts about the horse. Like the rules of the utility model, anthropomorphism is largely based on superstition. Fears, likes, and dislikes become part of a complex model of a horse's "personality" based on the human superstitious beliefs about how the horse experiences the universe.

- Superstition: A belief in things that are emotionally rewarding over actual facts.

This is very important, because we need to understand who gets emotionally rewarded by anthropomorphism: *the human being.* The reward is not logical or analytical; it is *emotional.* People love and perpetuate anthropomorphism because it gives them good feelings *about themselves. This does not make us bad, simply very human.* Benevolent feelings toward the horse can be applied in ways that fully support the horse's natural physical, mental and emotional needs as you'll see in chapters to come.

To fully understand how anthropomorphism works, I have created a set of rules that I have found always seem to apply to anthropomorphic situations. I have tested these rules in many situations and so far they have always been proven to work.

The first rule of anthropomorphism

*Anthropomorphism is **always** rewarding for the human.*

Anthropomorphic feelings toward animals are a human invention that rewards the human, by making the actions appear to reward the horse, *by that human's definition.* They may be based on kindness and benevolence and *may* actually lead to *positive* things for the horse. However, they may also lead to very *negative* things for the horse. Whether the horse benefits or not is **irrelevant**, because the anthropomorphic model is **not** about rewarding the horse *it is about rewarding the human being.* As a result of this strong emotional reward, humans become blinded to the truth; quite literally, their minds will reject or "fail to notice" things that are obvious, yet in direct conflict with their beliefs. This happens because their beliefs are based on superstition rather than fact, and because they get emotionally rewarded regardless of what happens to the horse. It is also why many anthropomorphic owners are confused about horses. You might also notice a similarity to the first law of coercion that we discussed in a previous chapter:

- Coercion is always rewarding to the coercer.

Anthropomorphism is damaging, ***because it is a form of coercion.***

The second rule of anthropomorphism

The more like the human environment we can make the horse's environment the higher the level of care is perceived to be.

If you were to construct a stable with imported wood, apple-scented grain buckets, a computer controlled central-heating system and import your farrier from another state or country, you would be considered someone who lavished eccentric luxury on your horses—wanting only the best for them. Everyone might agree with this, except your horse:

- Have you ever seen a horse destroy its stable from the inside out? The typical human response is to line the walls with rubber matting or paint the wood surfaces with something distasteful (bandage solutions).

- What about horses that react in dangerous panic to normal stable events and noises?

- Or horses that routinely scrape their teeth in an arc across a stall wall or mindlessly crib in a favorite location?

- Have you seen horses become aggressive and dangerous because they feel trapped?

- How about horses that do the opposite, seemingly giving up and taking on a frozen stare or becoming depressed robots that cease to interact with the world around them?

These are all counter-coercion reactions for prey animals. What would happen if instead of our bandage approach, we put our horses' reactions in the context of the species' basic instincts and needs?

Although we've all seen these reactions and more within the simplest to most fashionable of "horse homes," *most owners still don't understand what their horses are showing them.* These owners are not bad or cruel! Far from it. It is simply because anthropomorphism is a powerful mental filter. *As it constantly rewards us, it powerfully causes us to reject evidence seen by our own eyes and replace it with false reasoning.* From a human perspective, we are giving our horses everything they could wish for and more, yet when we fail to consider their simplest, basic needs as a prey animal, our horses must continue to react—first behaviorally then physically—eventually exhibiting stress-related health problems.

What can prey animals do to convince the most well-meaning among us that their habitat of choice is not one in which we'd be comfortable?

The third rule of anthropomorphism

*Because anthropomorphism is rewarding to the human being, it is **self-perpetuating** which means it will always increase.*

Think back to the positive and negative reinforcement training models for any species (Chapter 2). A behavior, in this case a human one, that is being reinforced will increase, so we are on the left side of our table. Another thing to note about this rule is that it is a variation on the second law of coercion that states that:

- Coercion will always increase.

Anthropomorphism permeates every aspect of our relationship with our horses even if your horse is very much a utility horse. There will still be a great deal about your relationship that is anthropomorphic. For example, whether based on human convenience or beliefs about a horse's safety, it is common for horse owners to consider a horse better off living under a roof with four walls rather than in a herd. This relatively quick and easy decision unwittingly leads horse owners down a decision path resulting in *more* danger and inconvenience rather than less—the exact opposite of what was intended.

The fourth rule of anthropomorphism

*Ultimately anthropomorphism **will give us** the **opposite behavior** from the one we want, despite our best intentions.*

Prey animals are programmed by nature to behave in a way that is opposite to a predator animal. When we impose predator ideas on a horse we will inevitably produce the opposite of the things we find rewarding. In a moment I will look at some common examples of opposing behavior or reactions to coercion, in this case, counter-coercion. There is a term used in natural horsemanship (see next model), that calls this type of behavior "opposition reflex."

There are many examples of the rules of anthropomorphism but here is the most common one.

Horses and stables

Scenario: An owner puts his horses in a stable at night most of the year. If the weather is bad in the winter, the horses are kept in for their own protection from the elements, often both day and night. The owner is rewarded by thinking he is doing the best for his horses. He has cozy feelings about how the horses will appreciate the warmth and protection and will not get too cold and risk a chill, thus he is rewarded emotionally because he sees himself as a caring and loving horse owner.

But a horse responds to this scenario oppositely to what the owners want.
The horse is isolated from other horses in an environment that does not meet its most basic emotional needs, *especially the need for safety*. Because its ability to escape the situation by *flight* is taken away, its alternative is to *fight,* attempting to destroy the stable with its hooves and teeth. It may well become aggressive and may even attack people that enter its stall. When it is finally given the opportunity to get out, it charges through the open door. After many weeks of this behavior, the horse gives up and becomes *compliant;* it switches off from the coercive environment and spends long periods just standing and staring, a situation in humans we would equate with severe depression but also frequently misinterpreted as acceptance and obedience. Frequently, this leads to a set of behaviors known as stereotypical behaviors, or stable vices, as the horse attempts to cope with its environment.

Stable vices or stereotypical behaviors include box walking, weaving, wind-sucking, wood chewing and cribbing, constant kicking of walls and even self-harming—all displaced fight or flight behaviors. Many owners see these as part of everyday life in a stable and although they are inconvenient they are frequently seen as acceptable, if not inevitable.

This scenario inevitably will lead to a case of counter-coercion or extreme opposition reflex—the rider will be thrown, the horse will bolt, kick, bite or someone will get hurt. Usually it is about this time the owner decides to sell the horse. Actually the owner is blaming the horse for being a prey animal, he does not realize the coercive force the horse is reacting against is its environment. I will look at the deadly implications of this in a later chapter.

How owners cope with this situation

Some owners feel quite badly about their relationship with their horses when the horses are behaving like this. They become confused because they cannot reconcile their enormously caring feelings with such obvious distress in the horse. And it definitely doesn't live up to the ideas of how it was going to be when they got the horse. One way to help themselves feel better is to go shopping—for the horse.

Treats and "stuff"

One of the most popular ideas humans have when they take up ownership of an animal is that the animal will always be an eager recipient of treats, toys and clothing—*material possessions.*

Treats are probably the most extreme form of superstition as they compound confusion and misunderstandings with potentially disastrous effect on a horse's physical health. There are caring owners who feed horses human foods: soft fruits, vegetables, even potato peelings. Needless to say, these horses also tend to have food or colic issues but because the owners are so rewarded by treating a begging horse, they are blinded to the potential and real consequences of their actions. Horses routinely die from what is generally diagnosed as colic and digestive disorders. But because this happens so frequently, owners don't connect *their* specific actions to the cause.

- Colic is frequently cited as the most common disease of domestic horses yet it is virtually unknown in the wild horse except in the rare event of accidental poisoning.

Why do manufactured horse (and dog) treats come in so many flavors? *Hint:* It's not for the horse's palate.

The reason the act of treating animals is so powerful is because it is so rewarding; it is pure anthropomorphism because the one who is being rewarded is the human. *(Rule 1: Anthropomorphism is always rewarding for the human being)*. When the owner is buying "things" they are frequently of an anthropomorphic nature, clothing, hair brushes, etc. This just increases the amount of anthropomorphism in the horses' world *(Rule 3: Anthropomorphism will always increase because it is rewarding for the human)*. Later in the book I will return to the question of treats and show you how to replace this behavior with the positive idea of rewarding behaviors.

The worse the situation becomes and the more the owner attempts to find a human solution, they consult vets, trainers, experts in this field or that, and increasingly turn to alternative consultants—just as we do when humans become physically or mentally troubled. When humans do this they are once more rewarded with good feelings about themselves and their actions as an especially caring horse owner, *(Rule 2: The more human the environment, the better)*.

> As before, I'm not saying this expert advice is not valid or not valuable, and I am not saying it won't help the horse, but for so many people consulting these professionals and especially buying horses material "stuff" is really a way of **trying to buy their horses affection** and make themselves feel better at the same time. Another side-effect of treating is that some owners see treats as a way of compensating for the failures in their confused relationship that can be made up for by the purchase of material possessions.

This is also an example of the fourth rule of anthropomorphism. The owner wants nothing but the best in terms of health and well-being for the horse but what they get is the opposite *(Rule 4: Anthropomorphism will ultimately produce the opposite result)*. They get a horse that despite their best intentions, is sick, depressed and likely to show severe behavioral disorders. Here is an interesting thought:

> According to the animal charity The Blue Cross: "During 1991 more than 50 per cent of horses were signed over to the charity because of their owners' financial or personal problems. Today almost ALL horses are admitted to the charity because of behavioral problems."

Does any of this sound familiar? If you are starting to recognize anything about your relationship with your own horse by now you might realize that some, if not all of your problems are due to an anthropomorphic attitude but it is very important to realize:

This does not make you a "bad person!" It simply means you are a very normal human being. Anthropomorphism is something that is both *natural* and *instinctive* to all of us, including me! The reason we behave like this is because we are following our intuitive feelings as predators who have a strong nurturing capacity. However, we need to stay conscious of our horse's behavioral and physical responses to the environment we create for them. It's very easy to end up accidentally creating the opposite of what we seek with our horses. Don't lose sight of the fact that anthropomorphism is a form of coercion leading to the inevitable side-effects of coercion. I am continually on my guard against my own anthropomorphic attitudes **because I realize no matter how satisfying they may feel, they will not give me what I want long term and may instead create a very dangerous situation.**

Once again I am going to give you my "bold statement" about anthropomorphism. Perhaps now you can see why I say it:

Anthropomorphism is the single biggest threat to the health and well-being of horses **and their riders** in the world today, despite the fact that it is based on human notions of benevolence and kindness.

The four big superstitions

Anthropomorphism is a deep and complex subject built on superstition, but to simplify and put it in perspective, I separate it into four major areas where the most confusion is found:

1. Diet and feeding

2. Housing—stables and stalls

3. Shoeing and movement

4. Material possessions

These are presented in order of importance. Later in the book I will look at ways of correcting all of these areas in favor of the horse, but for now, understanding the ideas in this chapter are one of the milestones in our journey to understand the relationship between horses and human beings.

Misunderstanding and confusion surrounds the rituals and superstitions associated with feeding the horse, leading to one of the most common causes of death in domestic horses. The idea of keeping horses in a stable is at the heart of almost all unhappy relationships as well as a great deal of sickness and suffering for the horse. The damage done by horseshoes is plain to see, yet we persistently ignore its effect even though foot and leg problems are cited as the most common reason for destroying otherwise healthy domestic horses. Finally, we'll address the bizarre behavior humans associate with ideas like personal possessions and unhealthy feelings we project onto our horses.

Later in this book I will look at a way of thinking about horses (a model) that corrects all these false ideas and gives us new ways of keeping horses based on much healthier principles such as:

- mutual trust

- cooperation and respect

- the physical and mental needs of the horse as a horse

At the same time, I will present a way of thinking about horses that still gives us a way to have all the great things that humans and horses can experience together and one that has all kinds of positive side effects not the least of which will be safer, healthier and happier horses.

However, before all that, please bear with me a little while longer because there are a few more areas of real misunderstanding we must address, starting with possibly the most anthropomorphic area of all—diet.

Diet

Obvious or not, these facts are of prime importance:

- Horses do not eat the same foods as we do.

- Horses do not digest food in the same way as we do.

- Horses digest food through **microbial fermentation** rather than a digestive system like ours which is based on chemical **enzyme** action.

- Horses are **prey animals** that forage food from plant sources available in their environment while humans are **predators** who went from hunting and gathering their food in their environment to cultivating the food sources they need.

- Horses have evolved to eat and digest fiber in the form of plant cellulose.

- Horses feed for up to 75% of a 24-hour period, *moving as they do it.*

- Horses do not eat "meals" and slowly digest them as we do.

- Horses' digestive systems are continually active because the processes within them are literally alive.

- Horses are not able to switch from different food groups and eat meat one minute and salad the next.

Those are some pretty big differences between how humans and horses process the food in their environment. Let's look at a scenario that is considered pretty much "normal":

Our anthropomorphic owner, wanting only the best, ensures that his horses get fed the best food money can buy. This is typically a compound feed that is high in ingredients the owner perceives as being of high value such as foods rich in quality cereals—a high energy component of human diets. The food has tremendous "eye appeal" in that it looks and smells attractive and is attractively packaged. Much of the olfactory appeal of the compound food comes from molasses that has been added, so he believes his horses will be sure to like the taste. The owner is also attracted to colorful ingredients such as yellow maize, green peas and beans. Best of all, this particular brand has been recommended by friends and is made by a well known and trusted firm.

As usual all the rules of anthropomorphism apply:

The owner is highly rewarded with *good feelings*, the food is attractive and appealing to the human (he may even taste it himself), he perceives it as both high quality and trustworthy—*more human is better.* Because his trusted friends recommend it he has no hesitation in using it too—*anthropomorphism will always increase.* But what about the fourth rule of anthropomorphism? *Ultimately anthropomorphism will give us the* **opposite** *behavior from the one we want—despite our best intentions.*

Despite our friend's efforts to provide the best food money can buy, he is running a risk of causing severe problems for his horses by providing them with a diet that is at best an imitation of a human diet and at worst a potentially fatal mixture of ingredients the horse's body was never designed to eat.

Our anthropomorphic, but dedicated horse owner ensures that his horses are fed twice per day—9:00 AM and 4:00PM. The menu consists of a concentrated feed and a small hay net twice per day. To the concentrated feed the owner adds some supplements he has read about, such as cod liver oil and some herbal "calmer" that is intended to modify his horse's behavior because they seem to be quite lively recently. Most of the time the owner calculates the ration his horse should get based on his experienced eye and the size of the scoop he uses to measure the food. The owner has no actual idea of his horse's weight but despite this he has carefully read the nutritional advice on the food sack and is trying to follow the guidance. The owner sees his horse as hard-working as he wants to get involved with three-day eventing so he justifies the high energy diet as being something horses need during their training.

I'm sure by now you can see all the anthropomorphic and superstitious ideas milling around in this typical situation, but this is a kind, caring owner. How can what he be doing possibly be bad for the horse? All of his horse's problems are related *to the owner's ideas* about diet, housing, clothing and shoes. However diet is such an important topic that it has been given its own chapter, Chapter 6. I will return to the question of clothing, shoes and housing in the section on the last model, the natural horse keeping model. Notice also, that everything about the horse's environment is dependent on the ideas of the owner, in other words, *the horse's existence is totally dependent on the owner's beliefs*. Horse owners find this idea very appealing and emotionally rewarding.

What is anthropomorphism, really?

To answer this question we need to look carefully at our quadrant diagram again:

INCREASE	DECREASE
Reinforce/Reward	Punish
Positive Reinforcement Add something positive	**Positive Punishment** Add something negative
Negative Reinforcement Remove something negative	**Negative Punishment** Remove something positive

Anthropomorphism is all about removing and in fact suppressing, the natural behaviors of the horse in favor of human interpretations of their needs. Consequently we are removing these *positive* needs from their lives. The section that deals with removing positives is negative punishment therefore, *anthropomorphism is pure negative punishment.* I said in the section on negative punishment that it was often associated with the removal of freedoms of some kind and usually connected with the environment, this scenario is all about taking away **the freedom to behave as a horse** and putting it in an environment based on the owner's beliefs about comfort and convenience.

Anthropomorphism or negative punishment is centered around the idea of stables (houses), clothing (blankets), shoes and mealtimes—all aspects of the environment we create for horses for our own satisfaction and convenience. Coercion is being used here in the form of an enforced environment. The horse will attempt to escape this through the use of avoidance and violence but enforced environments are especially dangerous *because they cannot be escaped by the horse through its natural defense of flight or fight.*

- The horse was never designed to deal with coercive threats that continue 24 hours per day, year in, year out.

It was equipped by nature to escape these threats through flight and maybe fight, in this way a horse has a chance of escaping the coercion and surviving for another day.

The terrible secret

There is one more side effect of enforced environments of negative punishment that I haven't yet mentioned—an effect well known and documented in the human world, just not yet connected to horses. Anthropomorphism (negative punishment), is the *biggest single threat to the health and well-being of horses in the world today* because:

- negative punishment is not only associated with environments and enforcement it is also associated with **sickness, suffering and disease**.

If you don't believe this take a look around any horse yard where horses live in enforced environments particularly livery yards or large stables and you will find that these establishments are constantly attended by vets, sometimes on a daily basis, furthermore most of the horses will receive some kind of daily medication. Some examples:

- The horses display varied symptoms related to suppressed immune systems such as allergies, skin disorders, breathing difficulties, melanomas and other cancers—suppression of the immune system is a well known reaction to stress.

- Other auto-immune conditions affect the skeleton such as arthritis, degenerative joint diseases—growing at a rapid rate in the domestic horse population.

- Increasing numbers of diseases are associated with dietary imbalance such as colic, laminitis, obesity, equine insulin resistance (horse diabetes).

- Increasing problems linked with, and related to, the enforced loss of movement, a consequent loss of exercise, and the enforced wearing of horse shoes. Disorders such as laminitis especially in conjunction with Cushing's syndrome are a good example. Cushing's disease is one of the most common diseases in older horses.

Note: Cushing's disease is a disease that has many effects but is especially associated with the hormone cortisol, (see below) cortisol is also known as the stress hormone. One of the most common symptoms of Cushing's is premature aging as horses and other animals that suffer from it have an appearance of a much older animal. Therefore it may not be quite accurate to say it is always a disease of older horses. One thing that all "older" horses have in common is that they have spent a much longer time in the same environment, usually many years. If that environment is one that is inherently stressful, such as an environment of enforced negative punishment, this would present a plausible causative factor in the development of this condition.

Globally Cushing's disease is one of the most common fatal conditions in horses.

- These are the conditions with physical effects but there are probably equal number of conditions that show the mental suffering of horses in these environments, particularly noticeable are growing cases of depression linked to what are now referred to as "stable vices" or stereotypical behaviors and a whole host of other vaguely termed behavioral issues, that are endemic in the domestic horse yet, as far as we know, are rare or unknown in their wild relations.

- Cortisol, also known as corticosteroid or just steroids is also frequently linked with depression and mental abnormalities in behavior.

- In nearly all these environments you will find horses on endless courses of antibiotics, pain killers and other powerful drugs, frequently producing further complications and side-effects unrelated to the disease they were prescribed to treat. We've all read the long list of possible side-effects on our own prescriptions but what do we know about those on horses?

- A particularly common practice is the daily feeding of pain-killers such as bute (phenylbutazone). I have know this to be fed as a matter of routine with every "meal."

- One of the many common side effects of stress that is also associated with suppression of the immune response, is a painful inflammatory condition in the muscles and joints, usually treated with pain killers.

Horses are becoming, sicker, especially with diseases that (strangely) ***often mirror our own***, such as diabetes, obesity, immune deficiency related diseases, arthritis and so on, just as with our society these diseases are all related to long-term unavoidable stress. Why is this happening?

Some science

These facts point to the idea that the environments we humans are creating are in some way contributing to the deteriorating health of the domestic horse. In the following paragraphs I would like to suggest at least one plausible explanation as to why this might be:

- Anthropomorphism is negative punishment.

- Negative punishment is defined as the removal of something positive from the horse's environment. The removal of positives here are effectively the removal of the freedom to behave in a way that is natural for the horse.

- The opposite of freedom is enforcement. An example would be isolation from the natural environment of the herd and imposing an enforced environment within a human-constructed building such as a stable or stall.

The effect of this is to isolate the horse in an environment of ***chronic stress***. Here is a dictionary definition of chronic stress:

Chronic stress is the response of the brain to unpleasant events for a prolonged period over which an individual perceives he or she has no control. It involves an endocrine system response in which occurs a release of corticosteroids. If this continues for a long time, it can cause damage to an individual's physical and mental health. *Wikipedia.*

How horses cope with stress

All animals and especially prey animals are designed to handle *temporary* levels of stress. The purpose of the flight and fight responses is to help horses deal with these conditions. When the body is under stress in this way, the adrenal gland increases secretion of the hormone called ***cortisol***, also known as the "stress hormone."

This hormone is really useful at these times as it gives quick bursts of energy when the body needs it during the flight reaction. It heightens memory functions and concentration on the threatening thing. It temporarily increases immunity levels in order for the body to cope with injuries and infections. It lowers sensitivity to pain.

Short-term, this hormone is a vital aid to survival. Long-term elevation of cortisol, however, can have detrimental effects *and horses were never designed to deal with long-term levels of chronic stress*. In other words, cortisol production and other stress-controlling hormones and neurotransmitters were designed to be "switched-off" when danger had passed.

Here are some more functions of cortisol:

- proper glucose metabolism

- regulation of blood pressure

- insulin release for blood sugar maintenance

- immune function

- inflammatory response

Higher and more prolonged levels of cortisol in the bloodstream (as when in a state of chronic stress) have been shown to have negative effects such as:

- impaired cognitive performance and depression

- suppressed thyroid function

- blood sugar imbalances such as hyperglycemia

- decreased bone density

- decrease in muscle tissue

- higher blood pressure

- lowered immunity and inflammatory responses in the body, slowed wound healing, and other health consequences

- increased fat levels as in obesity leading to, heart attacks, strokes, and the development of metabolic syndrome, for example, Cushing's disease

Notice how cortisol affects levels of blood sugar and how horses are now suffering from many of the diseases that afflict humans connected with sugar imbalance, such as diabetes (equine insulin resistance) and obesity. Notice how elevated cortisol levels lower immunity and cause painful inflammation in muscular tissues and degeneration of the horse's skeleton and joints—an example might be "degenerative joint disease." Many horses are routinely fed pain killers as a result of these disorders. All of these conditions are seen in horses and all of these conditions are on the increase. Just as with colic this collection of disorders may have many forms but I would like to suggest, *for the most part they are caused by enforced environments of unavoidable negative punishment.*

The connection between mind and body is well established in humans showing us that diseases that affect the mind frequently produce physical symptoms in the body. And the condition most commonly associated with chronic stress is depression.

Depression and stress

Cortisol production under normal circumstances peaks in the morning then decreases as the day progresses. In depressed people, however, cortisol peaks earlier in the morning and does ***not level off or decrease*** in the afternoon or evening. This is similar to the physical response of horses under constant stress in which the levels of cortisol do not decrease or get switched-off. It is agreed among human doctors that stress by itself is not necessarily a "bad" thing. We need a certain amount of it to keep us healthy and the same applies to horses. Doctors also agree that stress is not the whole problem, ***it is the way one reacts to it that is crucial.*** For humans, the way we react to stressful situations has an element of choice about it. We can choose to react in a positive or negative way—but we can choose.

However, horses kept in an environment of enforced negative punishment cannot choose.

Without the element of choice in a coercive environment, their natural defenses of flight or fight are of no use, yet they will still try. They will attempt to destroy the stable with their hooves and teeth; they will attempt to barge, or bite or kick their way out of the environment; they will develop coping strategies such as the disturbed stable vices or stereotypical behaviors, and when none work to free them, they will ultimately turn on themselves and may even self-harm. Ultimately their immune systems will begin to shut down and turn inwards on themselves. One of the well-known effects of mental depression is the depression of the immune system, leading to further vulnerabilities to viruses and infections which, in turn, further compromise the immune system. In short horses become sicker and sicker.

Although these disorders and diseases have many forms, I believe they have only one main cause: ***negative punishment in the form of anthropomorphism***. It is the deadly link between treating horses as if they have similar needs and desires to humans, the emotional reward inherent in these beliefs, and the setting up of environments which maintain the belief system. This is the root of the conflict between the prey animal and the predator.

In this way the natural behavior of the horse soon becomes the enemy of the anthropomorphic beliefs of the owners. As a result, some owners will have a hard time believing the benefits of allowing the horse to be a horse outweigh the pleasure received from pretending they share human needs and desires. However, there are some shining examples of the early adopters of this approach. Later in the book I will introduce some of them.

Anthropomorphism is a feminine idea

At the start of this chapter I introduced the idea that the anthropomorphic model developed after the second world war and replaced much of the previous utility model thinking. I suggested that this was due to the large influx of women into the equestrian world, so that the anthropomorphic model can be seen primarily as a feminine model. I want to make one more observation which is not intended to imply criticism of women because I fully believe women will embrace and lead the evolution of horse keeping and training in the 21st century. However, the anthropomorphic model is based largely on a natural—yet somewhat misguided—feminine form of nurturing. Once the nurturers in this world take into consideration basic prey and predator needs, and how both can be met in much better ways than the anthropomorphic model allows, they will be an integral force in creating the best new world for horses.

Anthropomorphism and money

However, before I get into more good news, I mentioned in the previous chapter that the (masculine) utility model was frequently associated with **making** money from horses and I also mentioned that people often compensate their feelings by shopping. I'm sure the following statement can be proved by looking inside most tack rooms: The anthropomorphic model is far more about **spending** money on horses (but you probably already guessed this).

As the anthropomorphic model developed, the horse world began to blossom into a marketer's dream, targeting the ideal combination of horse lover and shopper. Extensive equestrian catalogs "improved upon" the four superstitions from the largely male utility model to attract a more aesthetic, feminine, anthropomorphic audience:

- *Diet and feeding* expanded to include supplements and treats.

- *Housing* included more fully outfitted stables and stalls.

- *Shoeing* was joined by accessories and toys to inhibit stall vices and behavioral problems.

- *Material possessions* grew to include everything from tack made from exquisite leather to fluorescent materials, blankets of bright colors, varying weights and cuts, to all manner and styles of leg and footwear.

It's now popular for **both men and women** to combine aspects from both the utility and anthropomorphic models for their methods of horse keeping while tending to choose from the next chapter's model for training methods.

Summary Chapter 4: The Anthropomorphic Model

Anthropomorphism is the misinterpretation of horse behavior as human behavior.

The laws of anthropomorphism:

- Anthropomorphism is always rewarding for the human.

- The *more like* the human environment we can make the horse's environment, the *higher the level* of care it is perceived to be.

- Because anthropomorphism is rewarding to the human, it is self-perpetuating which means it will always *increase.*

- Ultimately anthropomorphism will bring out the opposite behaviors in our horses from the ones we want, despite our best intentions.

- Anthropomorphism is based on superstitious beliefs about horses.

  - Superstitions are beliefs that are emotionally rewarding but not based in fact.

- Anthropomorphism is negative reinforcement.

- Negative reinforcement is associated with:

  - environment

  - enforcement—the opposite of freedom

  - sickness, suffering and disease

- Enforced environments of negative punishment are deeply coercive and environments of stres.s

- The horse has built-in defenses against stress:

  - flight

  - fight

- These have an element of choice and escape but enforced environments are *inescapable.*

- Many common diseases are reactions to enforced environments of negative punishment.

- Enforced stress leads to depression.

- Depression further suppresses the immune response.

- This leads to horses that are becoming sicker.

- Anthropomorphism is a result of misguided nurturing which, once informed, will be a powerful force in the evolution of horse keeping and training.

- Anthropomorphism is a marketer's dream, fully outfitting the wildest dreams behind the four main superstitious ideas:

  □ Diet and feeding expanded to include supplements and treats.

  □ Housing included more fully outfitted stables and stalls.

  □ Shoeing was joined by accessories and toys to inhibit stall vices and behavioral problems.

  □ Material possessions grew to include everything from tack made from exquisite leather to fluorescent materials, blankets of bright colors, varying weights and cuts, to all manner and styles of leg and footwear.

- It's now popular for both men and women to combine aspects from the utility and anthropomorphic models for their methods of horse keeping.

Chapter 5
The Natural Horsemanship Model

The third model of horsemanship is a relatively new phenomenon only 20 or 30 years old. I believe natural horsemanship is a huge step forward in the training of horses because it has begun to change the focus of human thinking off of the human, onto the horse. To me it represents the hope of many horse owners to find a better way to be with horses, and it provides a way for many more people who have loved horses from afar to get involved in owning one. Simply the name, "natural horsemanship" implies there is a more "natural" way to know a horse—one that is based on the behavior of the horse and not just the requirements of the human.

Many readers will be familiar with natural horsemanship through popular systems developed by Monty Roberts, Pat Parelli and a host of others.

Although I feel these systems were a necessary part of the evolution in horse training, after many years within the natural horsemanship movement myself, I have come to the conclusion that they are only a step in the right direction, not the destination. I say this for two reasons:

- It is based on human systems.
- It uses the basic laws of behavior, negative reinforcement and the threat of positive punishment.

Let's look first at the ever popular human idea, "the system."

Natural horsemanship systems

Systems or method thinking is incredibly popular in human society and also something that has no equivalent in horse society. We humans love to buy into a system when we find ourselves in a potentially intimidating situation, and we feel much more confident if we can find a particular system—with step-by-step exercises and achievement levels—to put the horse (and ourselves) through. Because of the complexity of these systems, they can soon become the actual function for the horse. However, systems are not broad, general models of thinking such as the utility and anthropomorphic models. They are aspects and variations on those models.

Systems are great aren't they? Just follow the individual steps in the booklets, DVDs or podcasts and presto! You now have a perfectly trained horse and a perfectly trained and qualified rider. Well, actually no, that's usually not what happens. **Some** horses and **some** humans come through in the end but the number of people who enter the system is far greater than the handful that emerge at the other end. Why is this?

It is because systems are fundamentally coercive and *force* students to adapt to the rules and regulations of the system. *The system never adapts to the individual*, despite what some of them might claim. Let's look at a couple of examples of systems:

Back to school

The first is one we all know because we have been through it—the education system. The "input" into this system are thousands of individual children from all kinds of backgrounds, homes, influences, and with all kinds of unique abilities, skills and talents, in other words, *unique individuals*. In the UK the education system is defined as the "national curriculum." It is a whole group of rules, regulations, knowledge, opportunities and targets that over the course of twelve years is applied to children. The well-intentioned aim is to produce young adults that are literate, numerate and socially-skilled, ready to join adult society, and every academic year this system produces hundreds of young adults that are just this sort of person. The trouble is that every year this **same** system produces thousands of young adults that *are none of these things*. For these students, school years are not happy years *because the nature of systems is coercive*. You will see in these kids all the signs that coercion is being used: you will see *flight* (truancy) you will see *fight* (disruption, both physical and mental). But most important, you will see *compliance*, a minimal effort produced in order to survive. All of this is because the system that is put in place is, from day one, designed to force individuals to conform and adapt to the system. They have no choice in this.

Note: Just as the laws of behavior are universal so are the effects of coercion, they are not limited to prey animals. Were there any aspects of your own education that illustrate this? Were there any subjects you didn't like, so you didn't really make an effort? Were there any teachers that you disliked? Did you try to avoid their lessons or were you disruptive? Did you make the minimal effort to meet deadlines, do homework or take exams?

You're in the army now...

For the second example and to return to the horse, let's look at an old system, but a *totally* inflexible one. The military system of 100 years ago was used to turn raw recruits and raw horses into disciplined cavalry units. Once again, the input into this system is made up of unique individuals with different backgrounds, different abilities, different personalities and other aspects of individuality in both humans and horses. The system then works on the horses and recruits, driving them all towards conformity with the system. Flight (desertion) or fight (indiscipline) is never tolerated with severe penalties for those who attempt it. The compliant reaction was seen as an acceptable outcome as it was usually interpreted as obedience although the consequent minimum effort was also frequently punished. The output from this system was deliberately designed to suppress individuality through the use of enforced coercion.

What can we learn from these examples? We can learn that systems thinking—although producing a small number of successes—will also usually produce an even greater number of drop outs, unless the coercion used is extreme and flight, fight or even compliance is not an option. Systems are therefore **very inefficient.** Although a great deal is put into them, the output is minimal in comparison and favors only those students naturally disposed to adapt to it.

If we wish to use systems to train horses we have to realize we are using something that is likely to be only minimally successful, and therefore we are unlikely to be ultimately satisfied with the result. The odds are stacked against us, making it very likely we will ultimately drop-out (flight). We are using something that will take enormous commitment in terms of time, effort and money, and we are frequently going to have to overcome the instinctual reaction of flight, fight and coercion. Doesn't sound too promising does it? But we still like the idea of having a system to take the responsibility away from us. After all, if it doesn't work we can always blame the system! This is the reason you can find so many people who have tried a system only to have abandoned it. Many more will tell you, "I take a little bit of guidance from a lot of people." All horse and human individualities—and the possible pairings among them—won't learn best within a single system especially if it's rigid in its application.

Systems and negative reinforcement

The greatest weakness of any system is that, just like everything else, it is based on the laws of behavior. It is especially based on two of the laws that famously work together, ***negative reinforcement and positive punishment***:

- Negative reinforcement is when something negative is *removed* from the subject's environment.

- Positive punishment is when something negative is *added* to the subject's environment.

Note: There is nothing "positive" about positive punishment, the term derives from the sense that something is **added.**

You can see from this that because we are talking about either adding or removing a negative thing, the two laws work together. In fact they work together in the form of a ***threat***. The big problem with this is *both* people and horses find this to be quite upsetting. I don't have to tell you how you feel when someone expects your cooperation by threatening you. So let's just look at it from the prey animal perspective: First, take away the horse's option of flight. Now ask the horse to be cooperative and do something for you by using increasing pressure (threats) to "help" him figure out what you want. You're looking for the slightest try (this is where desensitized and stoic horses get a particularly raw deal). When you get what you're looking for, you "reward" the behavior by removing the threat. Hopefully, you did it immediately after the horse felt he put out the effort. If you did, the horse might breathe a sigh of relief, or he might lick and chew as he understands that although he couldn't leave you when you threatened him (unlike in the horse world), a minimal effort appeared to get you to stop and he got to continue living. Just as this sense of relief sets in, you decide you want him to do it again or do it more and you start the threats again. Do you think the horse sees you as a leader in his herd or a confusing, frustrating predator?

Here is an example I saw the other day:

As I watched some natural horsemanship students at a demonstration, the students were asked to use their "horseman sticks" to tap their horses on the ribs so they would (not surprisingly) step sideways, away from them. No sooner had the horses done this than they were pulled around by the halter to come back and face the owners. So what were the horses being asked? Was it "step away" or "come to me"? I'm not sure the horses knew and I'm equally unsure about the humans' understanding.

Confusion

> Confusion is not a good state of mind for a prey animal because it is one step away from making a mistake, and prey animals that make mistakes do not last very long! In this way confusion is also strongly linked to fear.

Let's look at another example of adding and removing threats:

Phases of pressure and yielding to pressure

The most recurring theme in natural horsemanship is that of increasing and decreasing pressure. It has lots of names such as phases of pressure or "looking for comfort." There are many ways of dressing it up but it is really the sliding scale between negative reinforcement and positive punishment.

A typical thing we might want a horse to do is to move back from a slight pressure applied to the horse's nose with our hand. Natural horsemen will tell you, quite rightly, that a horse can only go in one of six different directions: forwards, backwards, left, right, and up or down. So we apply a bit of pressure to the horse's nose with our fingers and wait for the horse to respond. It doesn't, probably because at this stage it has no way of knowing what you want, so we increase the pressure, say from "level 1" to "level 2." Desensitized horses may require even more discomfort to respond. At the increased level of discomfort, the horse might decide to respond by lowering its head downwards to get relief from the uncomfortable stimulus, but since that's not what you're looking for, you must maintain the pressure. There is no need to increase the pressure as the horse goes left, then right, or even up; just stick with it until the horse finally shifts backwards, at which point you immediately **release** the pressure.

This type of scenario is the basis of almost all natural horsemanship systems. It is the moment of release that is the reward and that is why negative reinforcement appears on the *increasing* side of the table. It might be useful to consider what is going on emotionally in the moment of release. The main emotion here is a sense of **relief**—a strong emotion for a prey animal and I believe much stronger than for a predator. Horses will quickly learn to seek out this feeling of relief as quickly and painlessly as possible by making the **minimal effort** to evade the pressure. Avoiding troubling things through flight is also something that triggers relief, avoiding a threat through fight can also bring the sense of relief.

> Because relief is reinforcing, it is an "efficient" learning mechanism in the sense that it works. Horses can be taught many things by quickly learning what actions bring them relief. Relief is therefore a reinforcement, but a negative reinforcement. It is a way of eliciting behavior to avoid coercive pressure which the horse does by making the minimal effort.

Negative Reinforcement in the form of seeking relief is the emotional reward for responding to coercion. Threatening to increase the pressure is a way of using coercion to teach what the human wants. My coercion test applies here: "Respond to my wishes or else suffer the consequences." All the side effects of coercion will apply and eventually the only refuge a horse can find is in compliance, which the human interprets to be "obedience."

> Once we understand this, we can see how we interpret what the horse is doing as "yielding to pressure" (obedience), but what the horse is really

doing is **evading** pressure (avoidance) in order to experience a sense of relief. It is also using **minimal effort** to do so which is a symptom of compliance. So in some senses teaching by using this method is a way of **teaching horses to be compliant** or as some behaviorists term it, "learned helplessness." This is one of the major arguments against natural horsemanship by those who oppose its use.

Why natural horsemanship?

You might be wondering how this type of training came to be known as "natural" horsemanship. Beyond the idea that once again, we have a predator controlling the behavior of a prey animal, there doesn't seem to be very much that is actually natural about it. But that is not quite true. Almost all natural horsemanship systems are based on original observations of horse behavior in the wild. One part of the natural behavior of the horse we predators particularly liked was the *horses' own use of negative reinforcement and positive punishment on each other.* We saw wild horses driving each other around, we saw high-ranking horses disciplining low-ranking horses by the use of threats, and we saw them doing this many times a day. So we thought we can use this to train horses because surely this is how they "train" each other. And of course, it can be marketed as "natural," "organic," "wholesome," "healthy," and "alternative," making it very appealing to those having a less than ideal time with their horses in the utility and anthropomorphic worlds.

Now please understand, I am not saying natural horsemanship systems are no good or that they don't work or that their use is based on cruelty and manipulation. They aren't, but they **are** based on **controlling** the natural behavior of the horse. Having said that, natural horsemanship systems have had a profound and positive, personal effect on the way I think about my horses and I remember their arrival in the UK as a breath of fresh air and inspiration, especially in a land where we were locked into the traditional world of the Victorian cavalry of the British Raj—where dominance, drills and discipline were regarded as the only way of getting horses to do our bidding. Natural horsemanship is a **huge** step in the right direction and in many ways it is the forerunner of what is to come. I think of these systems as a progressive stop on the journey to understand horses rather than a destination in themselves.

Natural horsemanship is based on controlling horse behavior

We humans have taken the fact that horses use negative reinforcement and threats of actual punishment—usually driving, threatening, biting or kicking behaviors—and we have decided this is something we can use to train horses, but this is not really what is going on. Horses do use these things but they use them *in a very specific way*. They use them to constantly reinforce *the rules of the herd* and herd life is based on an understanding of herd hierarchy. If you live in a society that is based on a hierarchy then you have to have rules to ensure that structure is maintained because without rules you only have anarchy. Anarchy would be a really bad strategy for prey animals, constantly panicking, stampeding. The physical and emotional risks of this would be ever increasing so horses have rules, and these rules are applied from top down.

Herd Hierarchies: One way scientists have of explaining hierarchies is quite useful. They assign horses something called a "resource holding potential" or RHP. The highest ranking horses have the highest RHP. If they choose to access a resource such as a particularly desirable food source, they will simply move in and take it from a horse that is lower in rank, with a lower RHP. This is the point when you will see negative reinforcement in the form of threats such as lowered ears, lowered neck, narrowed eyes or even biting or kicking taking place. The higher ranking horse will always get what it wants because of its higher RHP.

So what is the advantage of this behavior to horses?

The rules of the herd are enforced so often and so strictly because they keep *every member of the herd safe*. In a normal, balanced herd, as each member constantly reinforces and re-states their position and rank within the herd, everyone knows exactly where they stand and what their position is. They also can predict accurately how each member of the herd will, and should behave according to their rank in the event of an emergency. They know that in the event of a threat being perceived certain horses will act in certain ways and have certain duties, for example the alpha stallion will fall back to protect the mares and dependent foals. Non-breeding males will move to the outer edges of the herd to protect the rest of the herd members. In this way herd hierarchy and the enforcement of its rules has little to do with threats, aggression and confrontation because it functions in a way that benefits every member of the herd and enables them to survive.

A second point to make is that horses use the *threat* of positive punishment much more than the actual positive punishment. Continually biting, barging, kicking and so on would be little better than anarchy and would result in a herd that was continually injured from beating each other up. Horses are more sensible than this! By using the threat of these things there is a continual process of **assertive** behavior but not **aggressive** behavior and so negative punishment used in this way is a way of **avoiding confrontation** yet still maintaining the rules.

It is important to understand that horse society is not some kind of police-state and that high-ranking horses are always threatening and enforcing their rank on everybody else. There are many occasions during the day when horses socialize perfectly happily in a relaxed way with each other and it is common to see the highest ranking male playing happily with the lowest ranking non-breeding male. I call this a normal, *balanced* herd.

Negative reinforcement as communication not control

There is another aspect to how horses use negative reinforcement and it has nothing to do with *controlling* the behavior of other horses. It is all to do with *communication:*

- Horses use negative reinforcement to communicate something about themselves to other horses.

When alpha horses use negative reinforcement on lower ranking horses (lower RHP) they are communicating, not controlling. They are saying who they are, what their position is, what their physical and sexual status is, and the crucial point is, *they make their statement then switch off the threat*. There is no need to keep the threat going for a long period of an hour or two. The statement is made, the lower ranking horse acknowledges it, and moves away out of choice. *This is assertive behavior*.

Where natural horsemanship gets it wrong

When humans use negative reinforcement we don't use it in this way. We use it to control the behavior of prey animals because it makes perfect sense to us as predators, and we call the process "training a horse." We observed this bit of natural horse behavior in the wild, then used it out of context as a way of getting horses to do what we want. The big difference between the human version and the horse version is that when we use negative reinforcement threats, *we don't switch it off.* We use it to get the horse to behave in a certain way and when the horse complies, we change the scenario and use the negative threats again to get the horse to do the next exercise. The horse thinks, "I did what you wanted. Why are you behaving this way again? I can't win." (Sorry for the anthropomorphic translation). We then keep maintaining the threat for the duration of our training session. This is not assertive behavior, *this is aggressive behavior.*

This is why we appear to the horse as predators because we use our tools and energy to drive the horse aggressively, just as we would if we were hunting/stalking him. The horse thinks we are going to kill them. The idea that they should feel our release of pressure as a reward or relief and "Thank goodness you didn't catch and kill me this time, I look forward to the next time you try," is ridiculous.

This is why natural horsemanship and its related systems appear confusing as a way of training to a horse. It is because we use an unrelenting system of negative reinforcement and threat in a predatory way to get what we want by *controlling* the behavior of others. Horses use it in a specific short-term way to *communicate* assertive behavior and herd status without the use of violence. In most instances, they avoid injury, maintain the rules and keep safe. For this reason you will never see a high ranking horse use negative reinforcement to send a lower ranking horse around him five times in a circle to the left and then five times in a circle to the right because horses don't use negative reinforcement in this way. In the last chapters of the book I will look at positive training methods and return to the important difference between *communicating* and *controlling*.

Natural horsemanship is similar to hunting

This might surprise you. Many people over the years have been introduced to the idea of natural horsemanship and, as I once did, saw it is a huge improvement on the traditional methods of the utility model. But somehow I felt uncomfortable with it, and I certainly felt uncomfortable with the way some teachers and even "gurus" applied it. I wondered why this was, then I realized the clues are all there: firstly, natural horsemanship is based on a system of training or, put another way, on a series of goals. Typically there are little goals—exercises—and there are large goals—levels. This ladder structure is both logical and rewarding and makes perfect sense to our predator instincts because we are linking our training with our instinctive knowledge of hunting. *Hunting is the most goal oriented activity there is. Every hunter has a goal and every successful hunt ends in the achievement of that goal.* Let's examine the process in more detail:

GOAL!

You start with a goal. At first it is quite vague; you don't know the details yet, but the hunger in your stomach motivates you to go and hunt. So you pick up your weapons and set off.

Isolate your target

You go where the horses are, using your expert knowledge and experience of their habits, and select a target, usually the very young, the very old or the sick. You stack the odds in your favor by selecting a victim that is likely to be easier to catch. Now you start to refine your goal and you begin to stalk your prey.

Stalking phase

The important thing is to isolate the target from the herd and restrict its ability to escape through flight. Many hunters found that if they cooperated together with other hunters this part was a lot easier. By moving the horses around and driving them this way and that, you manage to separate the target horse. You then focus on the one horse and further refine your goal. You now have two choices: You can either work with others to tire the horse out, disabling the natural defense of flight, or you can maneuver the horse into a trap. Either way, your goal is now to get close enough to the horse to use your weapon to dispatch it. Whatever method you choose is all part of your advanced planning and based on the skills you have learned and developed over the years.

Success

Finally you corner the horse, and using whatever tools you have, bring the horse down and kill it, thus achieving your original goal and ensuring your

Mark Hanson

family's future for the next few days or weeks. At this moment as a hunter you experience the ultimate satisfaction. Not only is it exciting (the thrill of the chase), but you have achieved something your personal survival depends on. So this activity is highly emotionally rewarding.

Training

So why is this like training a horse, either in a natural horsemanship system or conventionally? Try this scenario:

GOAL!

All training is based on goals. Every trainer has a goal or at least an idea of what they want to achieve. Some trainers plan very elaborately and precisely or as we've seen they may be following a system. Some trainers work instinctively but all of them work methodically towards the achievement of goals. This is why people *always* ask you, when they find out you have horses, "what do you do with your horse?" In other words, what is your plan for your horse?

Isolate your target

You pick up your tools, usually something like a halter and lead rein. You go to where your horses are, say out in the pasture, you select the horse you want to train and remove it from the herd. Very few people would attempt to train a horse while it was still in the herd. You isolate the horse and put it in a corral, arena or round pen. Round pens are particularly useful as the horse can use all the flight it wants but the predator makes it easy for themselves and is never more than a few feet away. In this way the horse is trapped and under control.

Stalking phase

A lot of ground training consists of driving behaviors—moving the horse away from pressure, using advance and retreat, and above all, **controlling the horse's behavior**. With most training it is particularly important to attempt to have some influence over the horse's head and the trainer will focus the pressure using eye-contact, tools or body language to turning the horse's head, and thus its body in the direction they want it to go.

In almost all training there is a moment where the trainer comes close to the horse and may even bring the horse down to the ground, literally. I have seen

80

this done as part of the process of "breaking" a horse and in one bizarre case to "cure" a behavioral problem. It failed.

Success and riding

In many sessions the ultimate act is to mount the horse and ride it. Ironically when we do this we are sitting in the "blind-spot." The shoulders are one of the horse's vulnerable areas where horses are usually brought down by large predators such as big cats and also one the few places where the horse cannot see us.

Once again the *use of tools* is an integral part of the process and I won't go into details here but bits, bridles, martingales, saddles, whips, spurs and all the traditional tools of riding all have one thing in common, *they are all used to **control** the natural and instinctive behavior of the horse,* because it is in opposition to the natural instinctive behavior of the human.

So this is why many people are confused about the nature of natural horsemanship. It should be a great thing, and should have completely displaced traditional methods of training but it hasn't, and in its present form it never will because in behavioral terms both methods are based on hunting. This is why one of the main criticisms you will hear about natural horsemanship is that it produces horses that are in a mental state of "learned helplessness" or as I term it **compliance**. This is not the fault of the (usually) well-intentioned human but is simply an inevitable result of the process of hunting using enforced negative reinforcement.

Power, control and money

I now want to look at some of the common ideas that are found in all kinds of natural horsemanship systems, starting with "leadership."

Leadership

Leadership is a word used quite a lot in the training of horses. It is a popular idea especially with those trainers who have borrowed some ideas from the dog world such as being the "pack leader" and have adapted it to mean be the "herd leader." Dogs of course, are a fellow predator species. Leadership is also popular with utility people who train so much by correction, leading onto ideas of "showing the horse who's boss," or, "not letting him get away with anything!" All dovetail neatly with favorite (tried and tested) concepts like dominance and discipline—splendid predator ideas.

I don't really like any of these terms and try not to use them because they are ambiguous, which means, they mean different things to different people. For example, if I say to one person, "show leadership/dominance/discipline to your horse," they might go off and use really harsh language with their horse. Another person might go off and beat the horse with a baseball bat! Both people are wrong but both think they are showing leadership. So to clearly understand leadership and all kinds of notions that spring from it, we need to have a basic definition of the term. Here is my definition of what makes, for example, one horse the leader of the herd.

Leadership is the ability to control the behavior of others through the use of calm, assertive energy.

If you can control the behavior of other living things, that makes you a leader. And in human society especially, those who can do this are considered *powerful*. Therefore there is a second side of this equation:

Power is the ability to control the behavior of others.

So leadership and power are aspects of the same thing but notice that power is not always applied through the use of calm assertive energy. It can also be applied very aggressively through the use of violence and threats. When we attempt to control the behavior of another living thing such as a horse, *we are acting a way that shows our power over the other*. In human society there is a very strong link between the ability to control a horse and power. Think of the kings, queens, emperors and generals throughout history that have been associated with the control of horses as a demonstration of their authority. Even today, the ownership of horses, (when viewed as a form of control), is associated with power, and power is always linked with an idea we are very familiar with, **money**.

This link between power and money is very well known, the link is there because often, money is the thing that **enables** us to control the behavior of others, or as many of us are all too well aware, it is a lack of money that **prevents** us from controlling the behavior of others! We literally feel powerless.

When we consider some modern equestrian activities we can see they are very closely linked to money. Obvious examples would be horse racing, eventing, show jumping, polo, trotting, reining, and such. We can also see that these are all utility model activities, so this is why the utility model is linked to money—because it is also linked to power.

When we control the behavior of horses, we could be demonstrating our leadership or our rank and many systems encourage you to see yourself as the "herd leader" or at least of having a higher herd ranking than the horse (a higher RHP and therefore a higher level of dominance), but it is far more likely that we are in some way exercising power for our own emotional reinforcement, *because power and the ability to control the behavior of others is probably one of the most highly reinforcing (emotionally rewarding activities), we can ever undertake.*

It is very rewarding emotionally when we do it to our fellow human being but when we give in to our predator instincts as well and start controlling the behavior of prey animals, it is no wonder we are so keen on it.

Let's think about other activities that involve controlling the behavior of others:

- Any training is about controlling the behavior of others.
- All four laws of behavior are about controlling the behavior of others.
- Riding is about controlling the behavior of others.
- Hunting is about controlling the behavior of others.
- Coercion is about controlling the behavior of others.
- Threat-based training is about controlling the behavior of others.

These are all aggressive strategies and about power and control. We also have:

- Positive reinforcement training (more later) is about controlling the behavior of others.
- Herd hierarchies are about controlling the behavior of others.
- Leadership is about controlling the behavior of others.

These are assertive strategies and are about communicating something to horses.

Here is a list of the four laws and how they work as an aspect of controlling the behavior of others.

- **Positive Reinforcement** is when something positive is added to the horse's environment. This evokes pleasurable feelings in the horse *and* in the human—both parties get something they want.

- **Negative reinforcement** is when you take something negative away from the horse's environment. This is rewarding for the human (coercion is always positively reinforcing for the coercer), but it is also rewarding for the horse in the sense of bringing an emotional relief. One disadvantage is that the laws of coercion apply and coercion will always increase, leading to greater levels of threat and possible positive punishment: 'comply with my wishes or else suffer the consequences'. This training method is also highly confusing to the horse because even when it successfully produces the behavior that avoids the coercive stimulus, the whole process is repeated with the next activity. If that activity is "harder," (it usually is), the coercion comes back again this time with greater penalties for the "wrong" behavior. The inevitable result of this is the state of mind known as compliance and eventually a state of counter-coercion due to the fact the horse cannot win.

- **Positive Punishment** is when something negative is added to the horse's environment. This is very much the traditional way of training horses based on *correction* and is highly rewarding for the human. Doing the wrong thing always draws the attention of the teacher, in fact the teacher *needs* the student to make an error in order to "teach" the point. This is, of course, subject to all the usual side-effects of coercion. It is also the most likely to lead to physical counter-coercive side effects such as fight and fight also known as violence and avoidance. Potentially, this is also the most dangerous way to train a horse because of the physical fallout it evokes.

- **Negative punishment** is when something positive is removed from a horse's environment and is a form of coercion most closely associated with negative environments, unavoidable threat and stress. *Other links are with loss of freedom, loss of choice, loss of free will and force.*

Natural horsemanship is a masculine model

As we have seen the use of negative reinforcement is strongly linked to the use of positive punishment in the form of a threat. As we begin to expand the details of our original quadrant diagram we can see that positive punishment and the utility model are strongly linked and that negative reinforcement was a model of thinking developed by men for the use of men. Consequently, I describe it as a masculine model. In terms of our diagram, natural horsemanship is based on negative reinforcement and is the complimentary opposite of the utility model—also a masculine model. Although there are plenty of female students of these systems the original thinking, development and promotion was masculine. In this way the table begins to be balanced and symmetrical. Both negative reinforcement and punishment are used a lot in hunting and training and are primarily the tools and thinking of men. Here is the diagram in expanded form:

INCREASE	DECREASE
Reinforce/Reward	Punish
Positive Reinforcement Add something positive	**Positive Punishment** Add something negative UTILITY MODEL: **Masculine** Physical tools, history, tradition Practical, efficient
Negative Reinforcement Remove something negative NATURAL HORSEMANSHIP MODEL: **Masculine** Hunting *and* Training: goals, stalking, driving, ritual	**Negative Punishment** Remove something positive ANTHROPOMORPHIC MODEL: **Feminine** Housing, clothing, shoeing, diet

A negative world

When we look at the laws of behavior and note that three of them are coercive in nature, and we realize all the implications of the conflicting natures and instincts of the predator and the prey animal; when we see how historically the models of horsemanship have arisen for the benefit of humans at the expense of the horse, and we see how so many training methods and techniques are based on negative things, it is very easy to get rather depressed. When I first began to understand these things myself and started sharing them with others, the hardest thing I found was staying positive!

The truth is the world for horses, despite all the care, attention and money we lavish on them, is a very negative place because so much of what we do to this prey animal is based on what feels right to us as predators. This is not the situation we find with one of our other favorite domestic animals and fellow predator, the dog. All of these things also lead to the strangest contradiction of all and something that puzzled me for years:

All of this negative treatment and its side effects are inflicted on horses by **otherwise nice human beings** who are not cruel, cynical manipulators of horses, but people who genuinely want the best for their animals. They simply have never understood the horse beyond their own intuitive feelings.

Often these people are highly devoted and dedicated persons who despite having spent a lifetime with horses have never understood the implications of the horse as a prey animal, and levels of education don't seem to make a difference. Often those who work with horses in what we now know as the utility model may not see the necessity for understanding the horse as a prey animal as it wouldn't add anything to its function. But I believe the material to follow in the second part of this book will even change their minds. So before we get to part two, (and I've called it "the good stuff") there is one more area of conventional keeping that we must look at, diet. But before that here is a summary of the natural horsemanship model:

Summary Chapter 5: The Natural Horsemanship Model

- Natural Horsemanship is based on two things:
  1. A system
  2. Negative reinforcement in the form of a threat
- Systems input all unique horses, humans and circumstances.
- Systems are coercive in nature because they force the individual to adapt to them rather than adapt to the individual.
- Systems have very high fallout rates.
- Systems are very inefficient because a lot is input, but very few total successes are output.

- Systems are a form of negative reinforcement (comply with the system or else suffer the consequences).

- Natural horsemanship techniques are usually based on ideas such as "phases or pressure," approach and retreat, and yielding to pressure.

- The most common result is compliance (learned helplessness), often mistaken for obedience.

- Natural horsemanship is considered "natural" because it uses one aspect of horse behavior: negative reinforcement (it ignores many other aspects).

- Negative reinforcement is a way to control the behavior of others.

- Power is a way to control the behavior of others.

- Money is a way to control the behavior of others.

- Controlling the behavior of others in this way becomes *aggressive* behavior.

- Communicating is *assertive* behavior.

- Leadership is a frequently misunderstood concept .

- Training using natural horsemanship is a ritualized form of hunting behavior that will always lead to a state of "learned helplessness" or compliance in the horse.

Chapter 6
Diet

This chapter concerns diet and has been given a whole chapter to itself for a reason. In the entire equestrian world there is one area that is associated with more confusion, superstition, and strange mythical beliefs than any other, and that is the ideas people hold about what horses eat. I think this is because humans and horses are divided at their most fundamental level by the concept of food.

- Food is the foundational difference between the prey animal and the predator.

Diet is also the subject that attracts some of the most dangerous and damaging superstitions that can be found in the horse world, sadly, and the reality of this situation is:

- More horses die of "colic" than from any other cause.

Note: Colic is a general term used to describe an imbalance of the digestive system, frequently resulting in blockages, however, in reality, in excess of 150 different forms of colic have been identified by vets. However, I believe there is only one basic cause: *the fundamental misunderstanding of the horse by the human based on our anthropomorphic ideas.*

The real tragedy of this situation is that many of those ideas are propagated by the media and "experts" who benefit financially from promoting them. I include in this list (some), journalists, nutritionists, veterinary surgeons and feed manufacturers. Of course, I'm not accusing individuals but certainly collectively, these groups have quite a lot to answer for.

I have touched on the differences between the equine digestive system and the human digestive system earlier on in the book, here is a quick recap of the main differences:

- Horses do not digest food in the same way as we do.
- Horses do not eat the same foods as we do.
- Horses have a completely different digestive process to human beings.
- Horses digest food through **microbial fermentation** rather than a digestive system such as ours based on chemical **enzyme** action.
- Horses are **prey animals** who forage their food from the plant sources available in their environment (humans are **predators** who originally obtained food by hunting and gathering, and only much later learned to cultivate the food sources they need).
- Horses have evolved to eat and digest fiber in the form of plant cellulose.
- Horses feed for up to 75% of a 24-hour period.
- Horses do not eat "meals" and slowly digest them as we do.
- Horses feed almost continually *and they move as they do it.*
- Horses' digestive systems are continually active because the processes within them are literally alive.
- Horses are not able to switch from different food groups and eat meat one minute and salad the next.

Our part in this "horse-human equation"

The last point on the list above is the most telling because it starts to describe the digestive system of the human. Ours is not just a digestive system of a meat-eating predator, but it is the result of our own evolution as hunter-gatherers and later farmers. This means we have evolved to be able to switch to different food sources if we need to. However, there is one central idea we do get from our hunting ancestors and that is the notion of **eating as refueling.** This is why, in our modern world, we are obsessed with the idea of calories and nutritional energy values and GI indexes, etc., and this is why nutritionists spend their careers formulating complex compound rations based, not on the needs and behavior of the horse, but on numbers.

Nutritional values of foodstuffs are expressed as Megajoules (MJ) of energy in the UK or in the US as mega calories (Mcal) and recommended rations are expressed as Megajoules of digestible energy (DM) per kilogram (MJ DE/Kg) live-weight. In addition to this, compound feeds and feeding recommendations are sometimes expressed as percentages of body weight per hundred Kg.

Now I'm sure we all carefully calculate how much our horses need to consume in terms of digestible energy per 100 kg body weight. Or perhaps not ? Here is a little story.

A few years ago I did try this mathematical approach and wanted to calculate my horses' ration. The first piece of information I needed was an accurate calculation of each of my horse's weight. (This is quite easy to do if you make two measurements, from front to back, point of shoulder to point of rump and around the "heart line" just back from the girth. Then you enter these figures into an online weight calculator, preferably one that allows an adjustment for breed. This should give you a figure that is reckoned to be accurate within 5%, as long as your measurements are accurate!). It so happened that around this time, one of my horses developed a minor infection from an insect bite and I called the vet. She prescribed an antibiotic and was trying to calculate the dosage based on the horse's weight. I told her I could give her an exact weight based on my recent calculations. I happened to say, "I bet not many clients could give an exact weight like this," and she replied that in all her years of practice I was the only one who had ever been able to do this.

The point of this story is, that if I was one of the rare people who know their horse's weight and all commercial feeding recommendations are made based on a percentage calculation of body weight, then *most horses must be fed a ration based on pure guesswork!* This means that all the hard work of the nutritionists is wasted and undermined.

- It also means that rations are fed based on what makes the *owner feel good*; in other words their emotional beliefs.

As we now know the thing that makes most owners feel really good is *anthropomorphism*.

Some examples:

- Have you ever fed "a bit extra" if the winter weather is cold or wet?
- Have you ever based a ration on a handful of "this or that"?
- Do you buy or feed your horses treats, especially those based on human "treats" like sugar or cereal?
- Have you ever brought feed based on how *you* perceive the horse?
- Have you ever purchased food based on your horse being:
  - old (veteran)
  - young
  - thin
  - fat
  - breeding, pregnant
  - working
  - lame (laminitic)
  - breeding—thoroughbred etc.
  - sick

If you go to any feed store you will find a bewildering display of products designed to satisfy all these conditions and many more. So it is worth repeating:

- Most humans do not feed horses based on mathematics, they feed horses based on their own emotional beliefs.

We know this is true because we also apply this same logic to ourselves, our children and our pets. Unfortunately the result of this "emotional feeding" is that human and domestic animal populations are increasingly suffering from problems such as obesity and diabetes. We do this despite having more information to us about diet and nutrition than at any other time in history. This the power of our predator instincts.

A further point on the behavioral aspect of feeding is that diet is imposed on the horse, it has no choice in the matter and is completely reliant on the human owner and their beliefs to obtain the food it needs to survive.

I feel I am being a bit harsh on equine nutritionists they do a wonderful job, but their thinking is based on the idea of *refueling* and *calculating the energy intake* of the horse, just like a human on a diet, which is of course, both a predator idea and an anthropomorphic idea. It is not based on the normal feeding behavior of the horse—it is not even based on the natural diet of the horse. It would be possible to argue that, in *some* cases, it is not even based on the digestive system of the horse!

A better way

There is another way to look at food groups that is quite useful. Let's start with our human diet. For hundreds of thousands of years humans were a species that lived as hunter gatherers, much longer than we have been farmers, consequently we have evolved a digestive system that is designed to digest the diet of a hunter gatherer. This kind of diet would be things such as fruit, vegetables, nuts, roots and of course, meat, in the form of game, fish and poultry. I'm sure most of us have been on a diet at sometime or tried to eat more healthily and noticed how hunter gatherer foods we have **evolved** to eat would generally be regarded as "healthy."

About 10,000 years ago humans realized they could also cultivate foods and these cultivated foods are the form much of our modern diet takes. There are three main groups of cultivated foods:

- cereals

- sugars

- farmed meat/dairy products

Notice how all three are **high energy foods**. Notice also how these foods are all food types that if we eat in excess cause us a great deal of problems. Generally speaking, in excess, they are the "unhealthy" foods we must give up if we want to eat more healthily. It is food from these groups that are the root cause of the growing global epidemics of diseases such as obesity and diabetes. It is often access to these three food groups that are the main dietary difference between the so-called Western diets and those of third world countries, but most important of all, these food groups are not foods we have **evolved** to eat but foods we have **adapted** to eat.

So our modern diet could be divided into these two categories, evolved foods and adapted foods but there is one further point to consider. In the adapted food group they are all foods that are highly **addictive** especially when combined together. If you combine cereal starch/carbohydrates with animal fats you have the basis of almost all so-called junk foods. If you combine cereal carbohydrates with sugars you get things such as cakes, buns and biscuits, etc., all foods we don't really need to be healthy but all foods that we love to eat because they are highly positively reinforcing. We can see the effect on our own health of eating these foods excessively from the adapted group but it is because these foods are so enjoyable to us that we are bound by the law of positive reinforcement to eat them to excess. In other words, the more you have, the more you want!

Note: Sadly just because a thing is positively reinforcing it doesn't mean it's good for you. This is probably the only disadvantage to positive reinforcement...sorry.

The trouble is these adapted foods we enjoy so much are exactly what many people feed to their horses, especially cereals and sugars.

Cereals and sugar

Cereals and sugars, both adapted foods are at the root of all superstitions surrounding feeding horses and their presence in feed is purely anthropomorphic and the scientific evidence against them is growing daily—in both horses and humans, here is why:

We assume that because we can derive a lot of energy from one of our most popular food groups, carbohydrates in the form of starch from cereal, we assume that the same rule must apply to horses. This is wrong.

There is some historical basis for feeding carbohydrates in the form of starch to horses. Back in the days of the utility model a hundred years ago, when horses had to work hard for their humans, the high levels of energy that can be derived from cereals were used to supplement horses diets, typically in the form of oats. Many working horses did not have access to extensive areas of mature grassland and certainly were unable to fulfill their natural instinct to graze for many hours of the day and night as it would be a conflict with their "purpose," so the relatively economical energy supply in oats made a practical and efficient foodstuff for the working horse.

Note: Of all the cereal family oats are probably the "best" in terms of digestibility and are therefore absorbed into the body quickly through the action of enzymes in the **fore-gut**, (the first part of the digestive system including the mouth, stomach and small intestine). But this is not the part of the digestive system that is most important to the horse. The "engine" of the horse's digestive system is the **hind-gut** which includes the caecum—roughly equivalent to the human appendix—a large organ inside the horse where most of the gut microbes live. The caecum is not just large, it is huge! In a typical horse it is over 3 feet long with a capacity of about 6.5 gallons (25-30 liters). Another fact humans conveniently overlook about the horse.

The stomachs of horses are designed to process a continuous trickle of food and so continuously secrete digestive juices, primarily acids. When cereal is broken down by the actions of stomach enzymes, more acid is produced. Because these are not foods the horse has evolved to eat, much of the cereal content passes undigested through the gut and into the hind-gut. This acidic material considerably alters the pH of the hind-gut and kills many of the bacteria and other microbes in that part of the digestive tract. In short it unbalances the delicate digestive ecosystem (see below). This is the reason that adding cereals to a horses diet can actually have the opposite effect that humans intend. Instead of supplying more energy through the diet it can actually provide less because the "engine" is no longer able to function efficiently.

This is one of the main causes of 'acidosis' in the stomach of the horse and a major contributory factor to colic.

One of the reasons colic is such a danger to the horse is because horses are unable to do two things that almost all mammals can do, horses can't belch or vomit, therefore the horse's digestive system is effectively a one-way system this is why blockages are so dangerous.

Tricks and treats

We all like sweet things, it is probably because we are mammals and our earliest food (milk) is high in sweet sugary substances. Most mammals like the taste of sugar and horses are no exception. So here is a nice, convenient anthropomorphic meeting point: horses like sugar, we *love* sugar! So feeding sugar to horses must be OK then? No. It is disastrous.

There is a lot of well-known information out there concerning the damaging effect of sugars on the diet of humans. Some examples might be obesity, diabetes, heart disease etc., etc., and (strangely enough) these conditions are now becoming common in the horse population but it is not the chemical effects of sugar that I want to look at; it is the emotional effects of feeding these substance to horses and humans because as I mentioned these adapted foods are also highly positively reinforcing.

Sugar is something both species find **highly addictive**, this means, consuming it can become an extreme form of positive reinforcement. It is worth repeating that just because something is a positive reinforcement it doesn't mean it is good for you. For example, smoking, drinking, cream cakes and chocolate! The more you have the more you want. This means that a great deal of pleasure is associated in the mind of the human with the feeding of sugar, especially in one form—in the horse world we call it molasses, in the human world it is sometimes called black treacle.

Molasses is added to feeds for several reasons:

- It adds a great eye and nose and taste appeal for the human, who is thus more likely to buy it.

- It is an excellent preservative. Foods stay fresh longer, therefore you are more likely to buy it.

- Molasses is sticky and prevents the mixed ingredients in compound feed from separating, therefore the horse will eat up the less palatable compounds resulting in less waste so you are more likely to buy the product because your horse obviously enjoys it so much!

- It is very high in energy so we know it is a great refueling substance. As predators, we all know the importance of refueling, therefore we are keen to buy these kinds of products.

- It is high in energy and so allows feed companies to substitute lower energy ingredients while still meeting legal and statutory levels. This means it can help produce more economic feeds that are more likely to be popular sellers.

- Molasses is especially good at providing energy when it is *added to cereals(!)*, we know this is just what our horses need, so we are very likely to buy these products.

- We are probably addicted to sugar ourselves so we understand what a treat it is to buy these products for our horse.

- "Treating" our horse is highly emotionally rewarding for us. Which is why we like to do this and buy these products.

- Molasses is often fed with every "meal" throughout the horse's life.

- Because humans feed their horses based on their own emotions and not on mathematics or even scientific evidence, feeding sugar is highly rewarding to us.

- The needs of the horse, by the way, are irrelevant.

You might notice that nearly all the reasons above actually reinforce our good feelings about ourselves. This is what a salesman would call the benefits of the products. Whether a product is sold on its features or its benefits we must remember:

- Our horses are totally at our mercy when it comes to feeding them.

- As the field of equine nutrition is highly complex and specialized area of science and as the multi-billion dollar global animal feed industry has access to all the marketing and advertising resources of the human food industry, it is no wonder that most people feel slightly overwhelmed by this and consequently feed their horses based on the one thing they do understand—*what feels right to them.*

If you think back to the story about calculating the horses weight, you will remember I said most horses are fed a ration based on guesswork but it is much more than this.

- Almost nobody feeds a horse a diet based on science or mathematics. They feed a diet based on their own emotions.

The conclusion we can draw from all this information and behavior is that the human approach to diet and feeding is not one that benefits the horse's digestive system and is largely unnatural if not actually alien to it.

- Our own digestive systems are designed to adapt instantly to different food groups: carbs, fats, proteins etc. We can do this because our digestive system works chemically, based on enzyme action which allows us to eat, and enjoy eating, a wide range of different foods throughout our lives.

- Horses' digestive systems and appetites (as usual) are the **opposite** of ours in that they are quite happy to eat basically the same food every day of their lives. They do not need—and certainly do not crave—the variation in diet that we humans do.

This is important because human ideas about the right diet based on our emotions frequently unbalance the digestive system of the horse. This is the behavioral side of things, but what of the scientific?

Usually I try to avoid scientific jargon, so my apologies for the next section.

Dysbiosis or leaky gut syndrome

Dysbiosis is also known (rather alarmingly) as "Leaky Gut Syndrome." it is defined as a perforated hind gut, or ulceration of the gastrointestinal (digestive) tract, but in essence, it is the result of the gastrointestinal tract becoming "unbalanced."

Here is another bit of jargon: "symbiosis." When two organisms live cooperatively together their relationship is known as a *symbiotic* one. The relationship between gut microbes and the horse is just such a relationship. These friendly bacteria help keep the horse's gut in balance and also have other functions such as detoxification, vitamin production, and protection against diseases. When the environment becomes unbalanced (dis-symbiosis or dysbiosis), the number of bacteria changes rapidly thus unbalancing the environment further. It is this excessive bacteria growth that actually starts to eat through the gut wall, hence "leaky gut syndrome." Holes appear in the gut wall and allow all kinds of organisms and pathogens to enter the bloodstream. The horse's body reacts to this in the same way it reacts to other foreign invaders by producing not only an immune system response together with inflammation of the tissues but also an *insulin resistance response*. Essentially this is a metabolic syndrome characterized by an inability to transport glucose into the cells.

Here are excerpts from a scientific paper that describes the effect of this rather well:

This resonates in the horse because an increased risk of several digestive and metabolic disorders has been associated with feeding (high carbohydrate and sugar) meals of grain and molasses. Post eating, the pancreas produces insulin to lower blood sugar levels, however with the consequent flooding of sugar into the blood due to dysbiosis, this results in reactive "rushes" of insulin that either cause decreased future insulin levels leading to high blood sugar (diabetes), erratic insulin levels leading to low blood sugar (hypoglycemia), or Syndrome X, (Insulin Resistance syndrome), whereby insulin receptors in the liver, muscle and fat cells become damaged and cannot transport glucose effectively. These blood sugar conditions also cause the adrenal glands to produce increased cortisol levels catabolizing proteins and weakening and inflaming connective tissue and lamellar structures within the feet. The cells become resistant to insulin and the glucose from the feed can no longer penetrate the cells. In turn, the horse suffers from inflammation, laminitis, and/or founder. This metabolic syndrome also causes a general build up of lactic acid (due to stress and poor oxygenation) that interferes with muscle function, endurance, metabolism, immunity, and hoof health, exacerbating laminitis.

Once dysbiosis occurs in the equid (horse), this essentially opens the door to many equine diseases. In addition to the aforementioned diseases founder, laminitis, inflammatory diseases i.e. arthritis, and metabolic disorders i.e. insulin resistance; dysbiosis also contributes to Cushing's disease, endotoxemia, Diabetes mellitus, azoturia, colitis, inflammatory bowel disease, irritable bowel syndrome, infectious enterocolitis, celiac disease, bacteremia, Chronic Obstructive Pulmonary Disease (Heaves), liver disease, and colic. Most often these conditions manifest in the horse as colic, which is often recurrent and unrelated to management. Chronic weight loss and chronic diarrhea may also result from leaky gut syndrome.

The only part of the above that I would disagree with is the statement that colic is unrelated to management. I believe colic is *entirely* due to our management of the horse and especially the superstitious beliefs we hold about them. The final excerpt from this paper is the most telling:

Treatment and Prevention of dysbiosis is fairly straightforward and a simple way to avoid such grave consequences. **First off, return your horse's life to him. Permit your horse to be a horse as close to its natural state as possible. Relocate your horse "out" with ample running room, grazing, and companionship.** [my emphasis] Offer plenty of high quality grass hay and frequent small low starch meals. It is always best to prophylactically prepare/protect your horse's gut prior to any stressful situations: deworming, vaccinations, shipping, shows etc. Maintain a well-balanced feed for your horse with appropriate Calcium/phosphorus ratios as close to 1:1 as possible. Have horses teeth checked and floated regularly and try to keep the horse's daily regime predictable and prompt as possible. The more boring your horse's daily life, the better.

Excerpts from: Relationship of Dysbiosis to Insulin Resistance & Laminitis by Kate McBride

Source: http://www.theotherside.us/equine_wellness_articles_dysbiosis.html

Think about that last statement, at least as far as feeding goes: *"The more boring your horse's daily life the better."* To me that sums up in one simple sentence everything you need to know about feeding a horse.

In the second part of the book I want to put forward a whole group of ideas that come under the heading of natural horse keeping and I'm sure you won't be surprised to discover that they are usually the **opposite** of all that has gone before. They will show you how you can return your horse's life to him and how to construct an environment that is as near to the natural state as possible.

But before that here is a summary of the very important chapter on diet and feeding.

Summary Chapter 6: Diet

- Colic is the biggest killer of horses worldwide.
- Colic and related conditions are caused by an imbalance of the horse's internal ecosystem.
- Horses cannot belch or vomit, this makes the horse's digestive system a one-way system making blockages potentially fatal.

Diet

- Feeds are formulated based on their nutritional and energy content.
- Most horse owners feed horses based on their own emotional beliefs, not nutritional science or mathematics.
- Humans are familiar with the notion of "refueling" and mealtimes—predator thinking.
- Most emotional beliefs are superstitious and anthropomorphic.
- Horses are dependent on the emotional beliefs of their owners.
- Dysbiosis is an imbalance in the horses natural gut bacteria.
- Dysbiosis causes holes in the horse's hind gut.
- This allows bacteria and other pathogens to enter the blood.
- This has multiple negative effects on the horse's health, including laminitis.
- As far as feeding goes: "The more boring your horse's daily life, the better."

Part Two

The Good Stuff

For more than a thousand years

humans have taken the things

they wanted from the horse.

The 21st century is our chance

to give something back.

This is how we start.

Chapter 7
The Natural Horse Keeping Model

In this part of the book I want to introduce you to the idea of the fourth model of horsemanship that I call the natural horse keeping model. I want to show clearly how it differs from the previous three models and how it compares to them.

- All the other models (utility, anthropomorphic and natural horsemanship), are based on what is good for the human, in other words, what feels right to the human, and as we've seen, what feels right to us is to act like predators.

- The natural horse keeping model is not based on satisfying human feelings. Rather, it is based on *foundational principles* that give the horse what it needs, as a horse, to be happy and healthy. And in so doing, *we get what we want* because happy and healthy animals are much more likely to be able to give it to us.

- The natural horse keeping model is therefore balanced because both parties benefit, and it is based on positive principles rather than the exploitation of the prey animal by the predator.

I believe this is the only healthy relationship to have with a horse. By applying principles we can move away from ideas and emotions that conflict, and we can move toward much more positive methods of horse keeping.

This is because this model and these principles are based on the one law of behavior that works like this—positive reinforcement.

Not wild horses—natural horses

One important point to make here is that when we keep horses in this model, we are not trying to create a "wild" environment for wild horses, so we do not need 30 square miles of virgin countryside to do this! Like all the models, natural horse keeping is a human compromise whereby we attempt to keep our horses in a way that is close to, and in harmony with, their natural behavior as horses. As a general rule, the more humans move horses away from these natural behaviors (their ethogram—see below), the more problems arise; the closer we move horses back toward these behaviors, the happier and healthier they are.

Seven principles of Natural Horse Keeping

The following list is a set of principles to guide our thinking:

- Principle #1: Our management of the horse must always create good health and well being in the herd.
- Principle #2: We base our relationship on the Natural Behavior of the horse. That means: life in a herd, life full of natural movement, and a diet that closely relates to the natural fiber-based diet.
- Principle #3: Horses need to move. Constant movement any time, day or night is a fundamental right of the herd.
- Principle #4: Management is based on the environment, not just the horse.
- Principle #5: The opportunity to feed is the main daily activity—up to 16+ hours per day!
- Principle #6: There is always something to look at or do. Horses have a right to live in a stimulating environment.
- Principle #7: Respect the horse as a horse.

Just as with the three other models this model affects everything we do with the horse. For example:

- how we manage its environment
- how we feed it
- how we regard its veterinary treatment
- how we breed it
- how we train it

- how we ride it

These principles must be applied throughout its long life.

These principles should be the responsibility we accept as horse owners. By applying them, *we can still get all we want from the horse,* but the horse gets something out of the deal as well: The horse gets to live the life it was designed for, to be rewarded with the emotions that every prey animal seeks, to be safe, and to live in the company of other members of its herd.

This can only lead to horses that are:

- happier
- healthier
- **safer**
- longer-lived
- easier to train
- more emotionally intelligent
- more willing to be trained
- more rewarding for us to be around
- more "valuable" to us

These principles are the seven principles of natural horse keeping. Here they are again in more detail:

Principle #1: Our management of the horse must always create good health and well-being in the herd.

This is the most fundamental principle on which we base our thinking about the horse. Everything we do with our horse should stem from this principle; it makes good (common) sense on every level. Good health and well being should be more than just a principle, *it should be a right of all horses.* If you remember, one of the laws of behavior was particularly associated with the absence of health, i.e. sickness, and that was negative punishment (the anthropomorphic model), consequently the natural horse keeping model is the opposite of the anthropomorphic model because negative punishment is the opposite of positive reinforcement. Here is the table again expanded for the natural horse keeping model:

INCREASE	DECREASE
Reinforce/Reward	Punish
Positive Reinforcement Add something positive NATURAL HORSE KEEPING MODEL: **Feminine** Herd life, movement, choice, long-fiber diet Principles of NHK	**Positive Punishment** Add something negative UTILITY MODEL: **Masculine** Physical tools, history, tradition Practical, efficient
Negative Reinforcement Remove something negative NATURAL HORSEMANSHIP MODEL: **Masculine** Hunting AND Training: goals, stalking, driving, ritual	**Negative Punishment** Remove something positive ANTHROPOMORPHIC MODEL: **Feminine** Housing, clothing, shoeing, diet

There is no occasion where the human can justify anything less than the application of this principle. It is a policy that will lead to enormous benefits for both horse and rider. Happier, healthier horses mean fewer vet bills, safer horses, longer lived horses which automatically leads to riders no longer seeing the horse as a means to an end or a dumb animal we can project our feelings onto in order to make us feel good about ourselves. It will also give us a positive lifetime relationship with our horses.

Principle #2: We base our relationship on the natural behavior of the horse. That means: life in a herd, a life full of natural movement, and a diet that closely relates to the natural fiber-based diet.

Real natural horsemanship

Real natural horsemanship should be based on real natural behavior and so should be "holistic" in its approach. Strangely enough, the standard natural horsemanship model almost never addresses natural behavior! It rarely takes into account the horse's environment and its implications for the health and well being of the horse; it seldom talks about providing environments in which natural social behavior can occur, and it never gives advice on feeding or health because just like its opposite, the utility model, it is almost entirely concerned with goal-oriented training. This is strange because the state of mind of the horse—usually a direct result of its environment—has enormous implications on its ability to learn and its reaction to the way it is being taught. This is particularly important when based on negative reinforcement. The natural horse keeping model however is based on an understanding of all the behavior of the horse. It focuses on providing an environment in which the horse can freely show this behavior and is encouraged to do so. This is because natural horse keeping is based on the *ethogram* of the horse.

Natural behavior is defined by the science of **ethology.** Ethology is the study of natural behavior of a species and the scientists who record this behavior are called **ethologists**. The observed and verified behaviors are recorded in a list called an **"ethogram."** All the behaviors of a particular species would be referred to as the ethogram of that species.

Even though many aspects of the ethogram of the horse are sometimes inconvenient to our traditional approach, they are the foundation of a natural horse keeping system. Some examples:

If we begin to understand that a horse must always live in the company of other horses, this conflicts with our human ideas about protection within housing and stables. But by offering varied environments in which the herd of horses can choose their own shelter, we are moving them away from a system of negative punishment—where we force the environment of the stable on them—towards a positive system where the horse has choice in doing what is best for itself and for the herd. See Chapter 9 about track systems for how to achieve this type of environment simply and easily! We will see all kinds of benefits right away. The horses will be able to freely form social structures and hierarchies. Interacting naturally with each other, this will form a herd that is balanced both physically and mentally which in turn will lead to horses that are much more manageable, trainable and healthy because they are able to satisfy their most basic emotional need, to feel safe.

These are some examples of the many positive side effects of natural horse keeping. It is the opposite of the many negative side effects of the coercive laws of negative reinforcement, positive punishment and especially, negative punishment, where the ethogram of the predator is effectively forced on the prey animal. The previous paragraph demonstrates the first and second principles of natural horse keeping in action.

Principle #3: Horses need to move. Constant movement any time, day or night is a fundamental right of the herd.

Movement is not only a fundamental right of the horse, it is a vital component of a healthy body and digestive system. Horses are fiber digesters that need only to be fed on low energy fiber-based foods from which their efficient microbe-based digestive systems can efficiently extract energy. The benefits of movement and exercise are well known in humans and there is growing medical evidence to suggest that exercise is effectively a "wonder-drug" with multiple benefits to physical and mental health. Exercise does much more than just build stronger, healthier, muscles, bones and ligaments; it is also well known that exercise can have measurable beneficial effects on the chemical processes of the brain. Horses are creatures of movement. They were born to do it, they want to do it and they must be able to do it—*24 hours every day*—if they so choose. This is a way that horses can maintain and *increase* their own health and fitness—for free and because they want to. In other words, they find it emotionally rewarding because they are returning to their ethogram. What damage do we really do when we deny them this fundamental right, and how ironic is it that we do it in the name of "protection"?

The most profound effect to the horse from humans deciding they must live in houses (an enforced environment of negative punishment), is their loss of freedom of movement. The laws of behavior tell us that negative punishment is often associated with loss of health, an environment of positive reinforcement is an environment that **automatically generates health**, through natural movement and exercise in the fresh air and sunshine, with just the same automatic inevitability that enforced environments generate the absence of health.

Horses don't just need to move, they *must* do it to remain healthy. They must do it in order to digest their food efficiently, to maintain their physical bodies, to wear down their hooves, to stimulate themselves both physically *and* mentally. It is a fundamental right of a *prey* animal, a *flight* animal, a *foraging*, *herd* animal to move when it needs to. Horses that have the freedom to move at will, in the company of other horses, are able to interact and react to the environment around them in the only way that is natural to them. If we start to accept new ways of managing the environment of the horse such as track-based systems we will lose forever the "cages and coercion" approach that is killing horses (and riders), all over the world. Once again, humans do not lose by this, they gain by having happier, healthier, safer horses.

Freedom of movement is a fundamental part of the first, second and third principles of natural horse keeping.

- If exercise could be bottled it would truly be a medicine beyond price!

Principle #4: Management is based on the environment, not just the horse.

Horses are creatures of the environment and whether it is positive or negative they are also products of that environment. When I see a problem or a factor that I need to change, I only try to change the horse as a last resort. I always look at the horse's environment first and see if there are changes that I can make to it that will benefit the whole herd, not just the individual. For example, I might notice that one of my horses is getting too fat. Rather than singling out the individual horse and putting it on a diet*, I will try to find ways to *increase* the daily exercise the herd takes (movement), I will place forage in places where they have to go looking for it (foraging). I might also *increase the fiber* in the horse's diet by adding, say, chopped straw to the daily hay ration (fiber digestion). The effect of this is to have the horses work harder to obtain the same amount of energy, this is something that benefits the whole herd rather than the individual. Always treat the environment, not just the horse.

Diet in this sense, is an anthropomorphic removal of food through the use of enforced negative punishment of the horse's freedom to eat naturally by trickle feeding over a long period.

Principle #5: The opportunity to feed is the main daily activity. Up to 16+ hours per day!

One of the most common anthropomorphic misunderstandings of all is the myth that your horse is spending too much time eating. The truth here is that it is probably not spending *enough* time eating and an additional problem is *what* it is eating. The digestion of fiber to extract energy is a slow process and because the horse's primary defense is running away, it is not possible to spend hours of the day and night standing in one place digesting bulk, so the horse has become a "trickle-feeder," nibbling and foraging just enough bulk to keep the process ticking along while still retaining the ability to run away at great speed if necessary. This process is fundamental to the horse and takes up such a large proportion of a 24-hour period during which the sociable and gregarious horse spends much of the time eating in the presence of other horses. Therefore, to a horse, it is likely that eating is not just a *physiological* (physical) need, it is also a major *psychological* (mental) need. Horses actually show their relationship to others by the proximity and length of time they spend grazing with others. Study a herd of horses and you will see this in action.

In order to have a digestive system that is one of trickle feeding, the horse needs to have a system that constantly works. And because the horse relies on gut micro-flora to break down its food, this system must remain balanced for life. When we introduce foods that the horse has not naturally evolved to eat, the horse must try to adapt to them, but we run the risk of changing the internal environment within the horse and thus we unbalance the internal ecosystem. At best, this means the digestive system is constantly working to correct (re-balance) itself, at worst this could lead to a potentially fatal colic.

Principle #6: There is always something to look at or do. Horses have a right to live in a stimulating environment.

Many years ago I worked in zoos. Up until that time, sadly, animals and birds were often kept in dull rectangular cages with little or no stimulation and, not surprisingly, they didn't usually live long, natural lives. Fortunately zoos realized this was not a good thing, (mostly because the public noticed this as well and stopped attending). One answer to this problem was to turn to science, especially the young science of ethology, and to start providing environments that were far more stimulating—ones in which the animals could exhibit their natural behavior. In addition, zoo-keepers started a process known today as *"environmental enrichment,"* where, for example, they would hide food around the environment so that animals could return to their ethograms and spend their day hunting and foraging food. This has lead to happier, healthier animals that breed more readily in captivity. Movement and stimulation are vital ingredients of a healthy environment, and movement and stimulation affect intelligence.

Prey animal intelligence

Intelligence in animals is a complex topic but looking at it from a survival point of view, it makes a lot of sense for a prey animal to posses an intelligence that was strategically opposite to a predator. And much of our daily experiences with horses would tend to confirm that this is the case. One thing to remember about horse intelligence is that horses are very fast learners indeed. They are especially good at deciding whether something is a threat and can be safely ignored or whether it needs to be treated with great caution. Because they are prey animals horses take a great deal of interest in the world around them. After all, the slow learners or the ones that didn't notice what was happening didn't last very long.

This is the reason horses are so tuned into their environments and is why they possess senses that are much more powerful than ours: better sight (a field of vision that is more than 360 degrees), better smell, better hearing and so on. We don't have senses like this because, like most predators, *we don't need them.* We only need enough sensory information to detect our prey and the brain power to devise a plan to catch it. Horses need to be "super efficient detectors," the better the detection, the better the chance of survival. This is really the crucial difference between how a prey animal and a predator experience the world. Can you see how a horse that is confined in a darkened stable is deprived of sensory stimulus? *He is not just bored*, he is likely to be highly stressed. He is blinded, deafened and deprived of every sense he was born with to survive.

In 1945 a scientist called Donald Hebb discovered that rats kept in a stimulating environment were able to excel in learning tests. To cut a long story short, his conclusion was that animals that were exposed to stimulating environments became more intelligent and a stimulating environment actually caused the brain to develop and learn, in other words, animals in a stimulating environment became more intelligent.

How much stimulation does a horse that may spend weeks or months or even years of its life confined within a 12' x 12' stable get? What is really happening during those passing hours physically and mentally? And more importantly, what are the long-term effects on its physical and mental health?

The last principle

We do so much to horses that runs against their basic nature. Most strangely of all we only seem to reserve this particularly fiendish treatment for our long-suffering prey animal companion, the horse. Here are some odd ideas to think about that generally we would be concerned by the same treatment to dogs or cats, or other zoo animals or even agricultural animals. We would regard a similar lifetime of confinement as a clear case of unnecessary suffering:

- the horse is the *only* species of animal that may be legally beaten
- beating a dog is utterly condemned by society and in the media whereas beating a horse can be seen on TV every day of the year, in almost every equestrian sport program
- the horse is the *only* animal that may legally have nails hammered into it
- we find it unacceptable for zoo animals not to be housed in a rich, stimulating environment based on science to satisfy the natural behavior of the species
- we have almost eliminated he concept of performing circus animals as their training and confinement purely for our entertainment is considered no longer acceptable, *but the horse is the one species that is the exception to this,* often promoted as a "tribute" to the horse
- many people are deeply concerned with animal welfare in agriculture and consumers are demanding more organic, free-range and home-grown meat and poultry products, especially those where animals can be shown to have lived a "natural life" yet this is the opposite of the conventional way we treat horses

By developing ideas like the four models and showing people how the laws of behavior work, I hope to show you in the rest of the book *how easy* it is to change what we do to horses when we change our way of thinking about them. So the last principle is really the most important and sums up all the other principles as well. This principle is the key to enlightenment—the key to happy, healthy, safe horses—and it is also the key to **your own** happiness, health and safety. For that reason alone it is worth writing down somewhere you can see it every day. The last principle:

Principle #7: **Understand and respect the horse as a horse.**

Before we move on, I want to close this section by giving you a comparison between conventional horse keeping and natural horse keeping; the best way to do this is to look at the four main areas where the two systems conflict. First in the conventional world, then in the natural horse keeping model. Both areas of comparison can be found in our quadrant diagram.

INCREASE	DECREASE
Reinforce/Reward	Punish
Positive Reinforcement Add something positive NATURAL HORSE KEEPING MODEL: **Feminine** Herd life, movement, choice, long-fiber diet Principles of NHK	**Positive Punishment** Add something negative UTILITY MODEL: **Masculine** Physical tools, history, tradition Practical, efficient
Negative Reinforcement Remove something negative NATURAL HORSEMANSHIP MODEL: **Masculine** Hunting AND Training: goals, stalking, driving, ritual	**Negative Punishment** Remove something positive ANTHROPOMORPHIC MODEL: **Feminine** Housing, clothing, shoeing, diet

In the diagram we have two opposites: negative reinforcement and positive punishment are one pair; positive reinforcement and negative punishment are the other pair. In this second pair we have four items on the punishment side (housing, clothing, shoeing and diet) and we have their positive opposites on the rewarding side, (herd life, movement, choice and long-fiber diets). It is these areas that illustrate the differences between conventional horse keeping and natural horse keeping.

Conventional Management	Natural Horse Keeping Model
Housing	Life in a herd
Clothing	Freedom of choice and shelter
Horseshoes	Movement
Diet	Foraging and long fiber

In the left hand column are four ideas that are obviously anthropomorphic in nature. The root of these ideas actually originate in the military utility mode as most ideas in European equestrianism are descended from the military. When the anthropomorphic model first developed after the second world war it began by adapting the ideas of the time and so these ideas come down to us today almost unchanged from history.

In the right hand column are four opposite ideas that are based on the natural ethogram of the horse and these are some of the most important basic principles of natural horse keeping.

Let's look at some details:

Housing versus life in a herd

The contrast here should be obvious. Housing is a central idea of both the utility and anthropomorphic models and most conventional systems are built around this. Housing for the human is based on ideas of a central base (home) where the horse is protected, warm, safe and secure but this is not how horses see things.

- Enforced housing is alien to the horse and is the opposite to its natural environment.

Life in a herd is where horses have evolved to live and where their basic emotional needs are met, especially the feeling of safety. Along with life in a herd comes all the natural social interaction and natural behavior of the herd.

- Horses do not seek "warm and cozy" they seek "safe and sheltered."

We might think, "but I want my horse to be protected, especially when it is outside in the winter!" So we have a way around this.

Clothing versus freedom of choice and shelter

Do you remember our kind, caring typical owner of horses in Chapter 4? Here is another typical scenario:

In the summer the horses are turned out to pasture between feeds, (approximately 8 hours) but are stabled at night. If the weather is bad the horses are always rugged to protect them from the climate and from flies (his horses are becoming increasingly allergic to flies), or kept in stables until the weather has passed. The horses are turned out into individual paddocks where they can see and touch each other over an electric fence but they are separated so that there is no risk of them hurting each other. One of the horses has a condition called sweet-itch which is an allergy to the saliva of biting midges and so is always protected by a fly-mask and turnout sheet. During the night the horses wear stable blankets especially as the weather gets colder. The owner calls them pajamas. In the winter the horses are kept in their stables for most of the day as the weather is too wet to turn them out and this would poach the fields. The owner does not like them getting muddy as this means a lot more work to keep them clean and it ruins the expensive blankets. Besides this, all the horses have suffered in the past from a bacterial condition on their feet and legs called mud-fever. If the horses are turned out they always wear thick turnout blankets to keep the mud off of them and protect them from the weather, especially if it is cold.

It should be obvious but horses do not wear clothes

Humans do this because we have found that wearing clothes keeps our bodies at a regular temperature and allows us to adapt to environments we find uncomfortable,

- *but horses are not creatures of **constant** temperatures they are animals of **variable** temperatures*

In fact horses are able to live in all kinds of temperature extremes and in all kinds of extreme environments and are quite able to tolerate large variations in temperatures over the course of a single day and night. I believe that human-beings have evolved to expect constant temperatures because we are originally cave dwellers and later house dwellers and both these "comfortable" environments are environments of constant temperatures. Wherever you go in the world you will find that either the heating or the air-conditioning are set to about 70 degrees Fahrenheit or 21 degrees Celsius. Anything either side of this we find either too cold or too hot and we can deal with this by adding or removing clothing. Horses cannot do this.

- I am always amused when I see horses and cows in adjacent fields during the winter and even sometimes during the summer. The horses are all wearing blankets and yet the cattle, who are also prey animals, herd animals, flight animals and foraging animals, with roughly the same body mass, almost the same internal body temperature never wear clothing in this way. A farmer would be laughed at if he tried to blanket a cow. The only real difference between the two species is how we humans perceive them.

There is another aspect of wearing clothes though that is much more serious. Blankets on horses, especially when worn over a protracted period of time, represent an enforced environment of negative punishment, many horses get this "protection" for many months out of the year, the owners get good positive feelings about this because even though their horses are turned out they are still trapped within a micro-environment from which they cannot escape. This is especially inappropriate treatment of the horse when this policy is not based on the actual temperature and climatic conditions but simply on the calendar! In other words the horses are wearing blankets because it is winter, not because it is cold.

I once visited a yard where the horses wore blankets every day of the year, winter and summer. They also wore stable blankets (pajamas) every night of the year as they were always put to bed in their "bedrooms." Every horse suffered from skin disorders and other illnesses and every one had "behavioral issues." None of this was the fault of the horses, all of it was caused by the beliefs of the owner.

The enforced wearing of blankets for long periods is a particularly subtle form of negative punishment. This is pure coercion. Obviously flight is not an option, but what about fight? Have you ever known horses to trash their blankets on a regular basis? Have you ever found a horse that rolls in the mud attempting to rid themselves of the clothing the human is forcing them to wear? Or are they just trying to relieve the itching and enforced overheating they must endure until the human removes the blanket? When we take into consideration the idea that enforced environments are linked to poor health it is likely that these behaviors, that are so annoying to human owners, are an instinctive attempt by the horse to escape this environment and so restore health through self-grooming.

This brings me to another aspect of clothing, freedom of choice. If we want our horses to be truly comfortable in the outdoor environment, we should provide them with an environment in which that is possible. That means giving them an environment in which they can choose where they shelter. I'm sure most horse owners will be familiar with horses that stand out in the wind and rain and completely ignore the expensive field shelter the owner has provided for them. Far from being concerned by this behavior we should be delighted to see it!

I remember a story I saw about horses during hurricane Katrina, these wise animals had choice and so moved to the center of their outdoor area and ignored the shelter of the stables they had access to. The stables were destroyed and, had the horses been in them, they would have been destroyed too. Consider the normal thinking of most conventional owners, what would they have done when they heard there was a major hurricane on the way? They would have followed their instincts and locked up their horses in order to protect them, and the horses would have paid the price. Giving these horses the freedom to choose how they interact with their environment was the thing that saved their lives. I believe horses know a great deal more than we do about being horses.

Is blanketing always bad?

After what has gone before you might be asking the question, is it ever appropriate to blanket a horse? The answer is yes, but only for the right reasons and at the appropriate time and that will depend on the horse's environment not on human emotions. Providing horses have the choice of shelter within their environment most of the time, they will be quite happy and healthy without blankets, but if weather conditions are extreme—by which I mean they might reduce the horse's core body temperature—then it is fine to blanket them, but only for the minimum amount of time. As soon as the climate returns to normal temperature levels, the blankets should come off.

If you think in terms of the laws of behavior, then if putting a blanket on a horse on a cold winter's night adds something positive to the horses environment (comfort), then that is fine, but bear in mind the longer the horse is blanketed, the quicker you descend the slippery slope

towards negative punishment where you are taking away the positive
of allowing the horse the freedom to control their own temperature. In
this way time is the crucial factor that makes the difference.

To sum up, It is quite acceptable to blanket a horse to improve the comfort
of the horse in extreme weather. When it is definitely not acceptable is when
the blankets go on at the end of September and don't come off again until the
following April, this means that those horses are in an environment of enforced
negative punishment for six months of the year, purely for the convenience
and emotional satisfaction of the owner. Here is a good rule of thumb:

- Be very slow to put blankets on your horse and be very fast to take them
  off again— as usual this is the opposite to conventional thinking.

Horses should be exposed to the climate *as much as possible*, they need to be
able to do this, they should get rained on and muddy if they want to be muddy.
Sunlight is especially important in the winter. Their skin needs to be exposed
to it in order to synthesize vitamin D. To understand the importance of skin,
take a look at this advertisement:

There is a better blanket for your horse: The Equine Natural! This blanket
features all the technology developed over **millions of years** of research and
refinement. **The Equine Natural** benefits:

- fully automated, integral thermo-regulatory mechanism (FAITRM)$^{(TM)}$
- uses "seasonal adjustment technology" (SAT)$^{(TM)}$
- prevents overheating
- totally wind proof
- fully waterproof
- keeps your horse warm in winter and cool in summer
- **self-repairing, self-renewing and self-cleaning**
- forms a high level defense against bacteria, virus, fungal infections and
  parasites
- generates Vitamin D—just add sunlight
- resistant to physical damage
- covers the whole horse

- has no buckles or straps

- integrated mane and tail extensions

- constructed using 100% natural materials

- available in a full range of colors according to breed

- owner maintenance is unnecessary or purely optional

- will last a lifetime - guaranteed

Imagine being free from the winter drudgery of blanketing your horse. Imagine a technology so advanced that your horse itself can operate it! Imagine your horse wearing a blanket that gives your horse absolute choice over its environment. You and your horse can enjoy these benefits all year round with The Equine Natural. And the best thing about The Equine Natural is the cost, it comes absolutely FREE with every horse. ***The Equine Natural—anything more is inferior! Available worldwide.***

OK, so I made that up to prove a point, but the horse's skin is one of the most important organs of its body. It is worth considering some of its many functions:

- Skin is the largest organ of the horses body and is the first line of defense between the horse's internal organs and the outside world.

- It protects the body from physical injury, invasive micro organisms, insects, fungus and poisons.

- It regulates the horses temperature, allowing the horse to be cool in hot weather and warm in cold weather, it adjusts itself with the seasons growing long thick hair for the winter and shedding this into a short coat for the summer. The hair is also multi-layered helping it repel, rain, snow ice and sleet while still maintaining insulation.

- Skin clumps naturally form points which direct water away from the body so keeping horses dry in wet weather. Each hair is controlled by an individual erector muscle which means that there are millions of tiny control points in the skin.

- Skin repairs itself when damaged.

- Skin controls fluid levels within the horses body by sweating and preventing dehydration, it also rids the body of toxins at the same time.

- Skin manufactures vitamin D when exposed to sunlight.

- Skin exudes pheromones that both identify a horse to other individuals and also play a large part in sexual behavior and attraction.

- Skin is an organ that is able to gather data about the environment, (temperature, humidity, climate, weather conditions and many more as yet unknown or not fully understood). Through touch and a network of nerve endings this information is relayed to the brain, a vital function in a prey animal.

- Skin is an indicator of health, usually it is self-maintaining, for example secreting oils to keep the skin shining and elastic. Skin can also be a good indicator of poor health as well.

- Skin is strong and flexible and grows with the horse.

Considering that the blankets we put on a horse take away many of these functions, even if we do this with the best intentions, it is likely that protecting our horses like this will actually risk damaging their health.

Clipping horses

I have to admit this is my personal pet peeve and so I will try to avoid introducing a lot of emotional prejudices, but given the section above on the wonders of the horse's coat, to me, it seems quite bizarre for any human to want to remove it with mechanical clippers, especially as that usually condemns the horse to a long period of blanketing, confinement and enforced "protection" until the natural coat can grow again. There are all kinds of traditional and historical utility model superstitions connected with human ideas about the horse's function, and that is the clue as to how this superstitious behavior arose. When a horse is clipped there is always some vague association with the idea of the horse's *function*. Some horses will get a "carriage clip" although it is highly unlikely that they will ever pull a carriage, others will get a "hunters clip" and may never go hunting.

Probably the main reason people cite for clipping a horse is because they believe the "poor horse" sweats too much during exercise. My response to that would be that sweating is a natural reaction in all warm-blooded animals (including humans) to increased exercise. Simply disguising it with clipping so that the horse appears to sweat less is actually potentially dangerous. However, what could be more concerning is that excessive sweating is an indication of a low level of fitness. The horse is not sweating because its coat is too thick, but because it is struggling to physically meet the demands being made upon it.

In English riding with its strong military roots, a great deal of emphasis is put on the physical appearance of the horse (parades twice a day), and in this sense clipping is one of those traditions most frequently done for reasons of appearance—and because other people are doing it—but what it amounts to is an enforced environment of negative punishment, the horse has no choice. Arguments in support of it are very similar to arguments raised in the dog community before it became illegal in the UK to remove dogs tails for reasons of fashion—appearance and superstitious ideas about the role of "working" (utility) dogs.

Horseshoes versus movement

The next area of comparison we should look at is the subject of shoeing horses in comparison with freedom of movement. Horseshoes are another military utility model idea that has been adapted by the anthropomorphic model. Though it may not be obvious, horseshoes represent an environment of enforced negative punishment, with all the health consequences that implies. Horses have no choice about whether they are shod or not, it is purely something that is imposed on them because of what their owners believe.

It is interesting to notice that there are two organs of the horse's body that are constantly in physical contact with the environment, the skin and the feet. Both these organs transmit vital data to the brain of the horse, this data is crucially important to a prey animal and yet these are the two organs that we routinely isolate from the environment in the form of housing, clothing and horseshoes.

The debate about the necessity or otherwise of horseshoes is one that seems to constantly rage in the equestrian world, with claim and counter-claim going backwards and forwards on both sides. It is also a debate in which some of the most extreme superstitious beliefs and consequently some of the most extreme views can be found. It probably goes without saying that keeping horses within the natural horse keeping model is not compatible with the wearing of horseshoes. My horses are all "barefoot" and always will be. I consider whatever short-term advantages shoes may appear to give a horse in terms of function, they ultimately are a damaging, enforced environment which removes the horse's natural ability to adapt to its world, and so ultimately *must* produce horses that are locked in a downward spiral of foot and leg problems. It is a sad fact that this is one of the most common reasons for destroying otherwise healthy horses.

Horseshoes are the ultimate bandage solution

The internet contains many hundreds of thousands of images that show the damage horseshoes do to horses' feet. There are also many thousands of learned, scientific texts written by experts on the same subject. You can browse through ultrasound, X-ray, infra-red images; you can access thousands of color photographs, diagrams and pictures of post-mortem dissected hooves; you can read forever a growing number of veterinary reports and scientific papers, all of which describe the devastating effects of nailing steel shoes onto horses feet. Equally you can read thousands of success stories of hoof rehabilitation and advice on how to successfully achieve a barefoot lifestyle for you horse. This is in addition to the many books, courses, DVDs and passionately dedicated websites available to us in this age of information. There is probably more information available on this one topic than all the other diseases and disorders of horses put together, and yet, keeping horses "barefoot" is still the province of the "eccentric" fringes of the horse world; in the conventional world of horses it is still "normal" for horses to wear shoes. Why is this?

As ever, the roots of these beliefs lie deep in the historical tradition of the military utility model. When armies started living in barracks, as for example, within castle walls a millennia ago, they wanted their horses to be conveniently accessible, if and when needed, so they brought the horses inside and kept them in stalls. Previous to this horses had lived outdoors in herds and were free ranging so their feet were able to adapt naturally to their environment giving them hard, calloused hooves fit for travel over all types of terrain. But when horses were stabled, they lost the ability to move and their feet were no longer worn down by interaction with their natural environment.

Certain other conditions occurred as a result of the horse's new life in a stall, not the least of which were the consequences of standing in their own feces and urine for long periods. The natural movement of a horse through its environment meant that horses very rarely had contact with their own waste products but in a stall they were in contact with these products for much of a 24-hour period. Because horses were now standing around for many hours in a day, their feet quickly lost their natural strength and became soft and prone to infection. The ammonia from urine ate into the rapidly softening soles of the feet and most damaging of all, the "practicalities" of keeping horses indoors meant they were no longer able to access their normal evolved diet of long fiber, which is bulky and difficult to store. This was replaced by an unnatural cereal-based diet fed at "mealtimes" to which horses were forced to adapt. Although this diet provided energy in the form of starch, it was poorly digested by the horse and frequently so unbalanced the delicate ecosystem of the horse's gut that horses started suffering from potentially fatal colic, a condition further compounded by lack of movement. Because this diet was not natural to horses, it did not provide the same nutrients as the natural diet of long fiber which horses had evolved to eat. And as this new diet did not provide the nutrients the horse's body had evolved to need, the nutrients vital to the healthy growth of bones and hooves were missing.

- Starch-based diets are all about replacing energy and "refueling" the body. Not about health.

Because the hoof walls were no longer worn and shaped by the environment, they kept growing, so horses began to stand on their hoof walls instead of their soles and heels as they naturally should do. Even under these circumstances the hooves of horses still tried to adapt to the conditions of their new environment by growing a soft easily worn away horn that because it was weak, frequently split and broke off as the hoof attempted to adapt. Thus many horses came to be regarded as having "weak" hooves.

Within a very short time of confining horses for our own convenience, humans found that their horses could no longer travel over rocky ground and were frequently lame—effectively cripples. A crippled cavalry horse is no use, and **could no longer fulfill its function.**

Horses were used by humans at that time as a vital weapon of war. The survival of **armies, empires and economies** depended on the horse being able to both live in a stable and to move. The (bandage) solution blacksmiths of the time came up with was to nail on horseshoes to the extended walls of the hoof, this meant that previously lame horses could appear "sound" and so fulfill their function again. The effect of the shoes was to lift the already, soft soles and frogs *off the ground* so horses began walking on the metal shoes and not on their own feet. Horses' feet can adapt to many environments but not to *no* environment, and of course, a crippled horse is not "cured" by horseshoes; in the long term it can only be further crippled.

This is where the superstitious belief that horses need to wear shoes came from. People believe that a horse that doesn't wear shoes is not able to do its "job," and because historically the horse's function was so important, anything that allowed them to fulfill their role,—even if it meant a reduction in the health and ultimately the life expectancy of the animal—was considered acceptable. Horses "need" to wear shoes only if we create circumstances that prevent them from adapting to them by behaving naturally, but if we create environments that are artificial and damaging to their health, we are forced to take measures that are increasingly artificial and damaging in order to enforce this environment.

A superstitious belief is one that is emotionally rewarding but factually wrong. Horseshoes are the ultimate superstition because despite overwhelming evidence to the contrary, many still believe a horse needs to wear horseshoes— it is emotionally rewarding. An example of this is when a farrier removes the shoes from a horse and the horse appears to be immediately debilitated and tender footed in just the same way humans would be if they decided to go without shoes on a walk in the countryside. When the farrier puts new shoes on, the condition goes away, and the horse is perceived to be sound again. Humans will then conclude that the horse is no longer "crippled" and has been instantly cured. The owner is understandably concerned when their previously sound horse is hobbling around and is understandably relieved when the condition goes away after the new shoes are put on. So they conclude wearing shoes is *better for the horse* than not wearing shoes. This is emotionally rewarding and so the idea that horses need shoes is superstitiously perpetuated and becomes part of the owner's belief system. This is then further compounded by hundreds of years of tradition that tell the owner this is the "right" thing to believe.

But as the evidence tells us, this is factually wrong because the horse still has feet that cannot cope with the environment. It is a tribute to the the eccentric fringes who have taken the shoes from their horses and waited patiently for the hooves to change and adapt, to those people who understand that a diet should provide what the horse needs to be healthy not just to be refueled for the next job the horse has to do. It is a tribute to those who bucked the trend, changed their thinking and believe a horse can live a natural life yet still work in partnership with human beings. Most of all, it is a tribute to those who sacrificed their own emotional superstitions in order to return the horse to a state of health and well being they believe is its birthright. This is why shoeing horses has no place in natural horse keeping.

There is another disadvantage to shoes that makes them incompatible with natural horse keeping and that is the horse's environment has to be one which incorporates natural, healthy movement. Horseshoes wear out.

- It seems ironic, that a lifestyle of natural movement actually conflicts with the use of horseshoes.

Natural movement is what makes healthy horses, we all know and understand the positive benefits of exercise and it is this traveling ability, this inward healthy glow that wild horses have, that first attracted us to the natural athletic ability of the horse. The horse has a body that is perfectly equipped to live like this and it is particularly equipped with amazing feet that can carry it over any terrain, but the feet are only amazing if they are allowed to adapt naturally. This is the function that horseshoes take away by preventing all adaptation to the environment by the horses' feet. Horses' feet should be allowed to regenerate themselves naturally to give a constant experience of the environment to the horse. Horseshoes are always in the process of incremental wear, providing a constantly changing experience of the environment to the horse. This requires other parts of a horse's body to constantly, incrementally compensate.

There are also two further factors that affect horse's feet: the *trim* that a good barefoot trimmer will put on the feet, and *diet*—probably the most important factor of all that influences the health of a horse's foot.

Diet in natural horse keeping

In natural horse keeping we take a very different approach to diet from that of conventional horse keeping. I use my own horses to illustrate this.

- The first difference is that horses are never fed in the "home" i.e., in stables, consequently they do not get fed "meals."

- My horses *are* given a bucket feed twice per day but this does ***not*** represent an intake of nutrients or a regular mealtime, it is simply a balance to their natural diet of long fiber and consists of more fiber and vitamins and minerals.

- My horses live on a diet of long fiber that they discover through traveling around their environment **as their primary food source.**

- My horses are never confined or tied up when they are eating; they always eat together and are able to show all their natural herd dynamic, so if a dominant horse moves in and takes the food of a lower ranking horse that is fine, that is his job.

- *I do not calculate rations because it is not intended to provide energy, so I give all horses the same supplementary feed regardless of size or breed.*

- I always present bucket feeds to the herd in order of herd hierarchy (or RHP) starting with the alpha male, alpha female, then mid ranking horses and finally low ranking horses.

- I have never seen a lower ranking horse take the food of a higher ranking horse, it will never happen.

- When the bucket feed is finished the herd returns to the track and resumes eating either hay, mature grass or haylage.

- This approach minimizes stress, avoids conflict and gets the horses back into their environment as fast as possible.

Many years ago I used to work in a busy riding stable with forty horses, all of which were tied up and confined within stables or tied up in the yard. "Lunchtime" was quite a performance as this was the time when the level of behavioral problems and stereotypical behaviors were at their highest. The noise from the "knockers" and the "neighers" and the "swayers" was at its worst. **All of these are highly abnormal behaviors.** Bucket feeding, far from being the quiet, gentle affair it is with my horses, was actually a time of acute stress for horses and humans alike.

Long fiber

I have mentioned the term long fiber several times, and I use it to describe various forages in their natural form, such as hay, haylage (preserved grass) and mature field grasses. Short fiber is usually processed in some way, for example through chopping but can also include by-products such as denatured sugar beet. All fibers however are forms of plant cellulose.

You might be wondering what I actually feed my horses in a bucket and why I don't need to calculate a ration. The answer is simple: I feed a mixture of five ingredients, the main one of which is **denatured** sugar beet pulp. Notice the word denatured, meaning sugar beet *without* the sugar. Essentially this is what is left after the sugar has been extracted leaving *more plant cellulose or fiber.* This represents the main bulk of the supplementary feed I give my horses. To this I add *small* amounts of:

- A great source of natural vitamins and minerals such as copper, zinc, selenium and iodine which are often lacking in a forage-only diet and are conveniently combined for us in a natural form—seaweed.

- Seaweed is easily fermented by the horse's gut bacteria.

- Ground linseed meal* (see warning below), high in an amino acid called lysine that if not present limits levels of other essential amino acids.

- Linseed* is a good source of omega-3 fatty acids which provide an anti-inflammatory function in the horses body.

- The oil content also helps coat and general body condition.

- Linseed* also has a beneficial effect on gut lining.

- Garlic** flakes, a natural antibiotic and blood conditioner and has many other health benefits, including antiseptic, anti-inflammatory and antibiotic effects.

- Garlic** reduces blood pressure, improves respiratory problems and even acts as a fly repellent.

- The only other ingredient I give is magnesium oxide either in a powder added to the ration or in the form of mineral licks that the horses have free access to all the time. Magnesium is essential for all livestock eating a long fiber based diet and is especially important for barefoot horses as it helps build healthy teeth, bones and hooves.

- Magnesium is frequently marketed as a calming agent for horses but this is not why I feed it because my horses are already calm. It is interesting to note that magnesium *deficiency* has been linked to laminitis, muscle stiffness and a depressed immune system, also well known symptoms of stress.

That is all, and is as complex as feeding ever needs to be as long as it is fed in conjunction with long fiber. My horses have lived quite happily on this ration now for several years and have never looked healthier. They have healthy coats, good muscle tone and strong hooves. They don't lose condition in the winter and they don't gain unhealthy amounts of weight in the spring. They never eat spring grass (see Chapter 9, track systems). They don't suffer from skin allergies, respiratory problems, obesity or any of the other anthropomorphic diseases. One of my horses suffered from most of these conditions when he was donated to my herd. The change in diet has been one of the main reasons he is now a totally healthy horse. But it was not only the diet that was important, it was the change in environment that set him on the road to recovery (Principle #4: Change the environment, not the horse).

- ***Please note linseed is an excellent feed but must always be fed in a cooked form**. Raw linseed is poisonous and actually contains hydrogen cyanide! Cooking removes this. It is perfectly safe to feed in a cooked (processed) form.

- **** Please note garlic is only to be fed in very small amounts, in excess it can cause anemia.**

This diet is one that is particularly good for barefoot horses, living a stress-free, natural life. It is also a diet that promotes a healthy life for my horses. It is easy to feed because individual calculations of rations do not need to be made (not fed to provide energy). Above all it is not a "meal," it is a supplement to their main food source of long fiber and therefore a balance to their whole diet.

That concludes the section on diet and feeding and the principles of natural horse keeping.

Summary Chapter 7: The Natural Horse Keeping Model

It's not about *wild* horse keeping, it's about *natural* horse keeping.

- The seven principles of natural horse keeping:
  - Principle #1: Our management of the horse must always create good

health and well-being in the herd.

- Principle #2: We base our relationship on the natural behavior of the horse. That means: Life in a herd, full of natural movement and a diet that closely relates to their natural fiber-based diet.
- Principle #3: Horses need to move. Constant movement any time, day or night is a fundamental right of the herd.
- Principle #4: Management is based on the environment, not just the horse.
- Principle #5: The opportunity to feed is the main daily activity. Up to 16 hours + per day!
- Principle #6: There is always something to look at or do. Horses have a right to live in a stimulating environment.
- Principle #7: Respect the horse as a horse.
- Natural horse keeping is a holistic approach.
- Prey animal intelligence is the opposite of predator intelligence.
- Enforced housing is alien to the horse and is the opposite to its natural environment.
- Clothing versus freedom of choice and shelter: Horses do not seek "warm and cozy" they seek "safe and sheltered."
- Horseshoes are an enforced environment which removes the horse's natural ability to adapt to its world.
- Diet versus foraging, the only feed given is a supplementary balancer to the whole diet.
- Horses are fed in a way that allows them to show normal horse behavior, i.e., never tied up or restrained.
- Sugar and cereals are never fed.
- Molasses—the big one! Completely alien to the horse and should have no part in its diet.
- Natural horse feeding is based on feeding the diet horses have evolved to eat rather than a diet to which they are forced to adapt.

Chapter 8
The Environment

In this chapter I want to start us thinking about something new and I want to start thinking about turning the tables a little bit, *in favor of the horse*. So for the moment, let's forget everything we know about stables, tradition, anthropomorphism, what works and what doesn't, the "right" way or "wrong" way, and start again with a clean slate, looking at the horse with fresh eyes. One of my principles of natural horse keeping states that we should change the environment and not the horse. This chapter will illustrate this principle very well. If we can understand the environment of the horse we can deduce what things that environment supplies and we can start to design management systems that meet those needs, so this chapter is mostly about the "needs" of the horse both as an individual and as a member of a herd.

Environments and "needs"

First we need to ask ourselves what the ideal horse environment is. It is, of course, a very different environment from ours.

- Horses live in herds, within a home range, not in houses.

Secondly, we need to ask how this environment meets the horse's **needs?**

The home range

The horse's home range is an environment where horses find everything they want for the continuation of the herd and all the resources they need for a long, happy, healthy lives.

- This makes the home range an environment based on positive reinforcement.

For example, if a horse feels thirsty, he finds water and so is positively reinforced when he drinks. This idea of finding a resource and fulfilling a need is the natural environment of an animal that forages for the things it needs to stay healthy.

But the home range supplies a lot more than just obvious physical things such as shelter, food or water. It also supplies all the mental, emotional and—who is not to say—spiritual elements a herd needs to live fulfilled, happy lives. The home range contains all of these elements because it is a holistic environment supplying **all** needs, whatever they may be. Here are the needs (as we presently understand them) that are satisfied by the horse's environment.

Personal needs

- **Personal Safety:** The environment must satisfy the *basic emotional need* for safety because safety is the main reason horses live in herds, because they are prey animals.

- **Movement:** Horses are creatures of movement; exercise is vital to their physical and mental health. Horses are flight animals and traveling animals.

- **Food and drink:** Only after the needs of safety and movement are met is the need to eat and drink important to horses. Horses are foraging animals that eat and move on at the same time. Therefore, they live in an environment that complements their method of feeding.

- **Rest and sleep:** This includes the need to find shelter from the elements if needed. The ability to sleep is based on having the emotional safety of the herd around them.

- **Body care:** Anthropomorphic owners spend a great deal of time grooming horses but it is a basic need of the horse to be free to roll and scratch, to groom each other, and to cover themselves in mud if they wish! Another aspect of body care is the ability to self-medicate, to find the minerals, vitamins, herbs and plant material they need to keep their body healthy. Once again, the environment in which they live satisfies not only physical but mental health needs of the individual and the herd.

In short the environment provides everything an individual horse needs to be mentally and physically healthy.

Social/herd needs

- **Socializing within a stable herd:** Horses are highly sociable and gregarious animals because they are herd animals. They need the presence of other horses to feel safe. Interaction with, and knowledge of, other horses in the herd is vital in the event of an emergency.

- **Play:** Horses are an unusual species in that, like humans, they play throughout their lives, play has many functions in an intelligent animal like the horse but is frequently used as a rehearsal for events in later life such as adult sexual behavior or competition in males. It is therefore a form of learning and vital to the stimulation and mental health of the horse.

- **Territory and Exploration:** Having an intimate knowledge of the home range is essential for a prey animal because it gives them an advantage over predators. Horses eagerly explore and learn everything they can about the environment in which they live. As usual, this is because of their nature as prey animals and is knowledge that one day, may save their life.

- **Feeding and drinking:** I place this function at the bottom of the list because although it is obviously a physical necessity, it is in many ways a much less important aspect of herd life. Horses do not gather at mealtimes to feed—they feed constantly. Horses do not come to a central area to rest and digest meals—they move and forage constantly. Horses are not able to spend 8 hours or more resting up or sleeping after a big feed—they are constantly on the alert to potential predators all day and all night. They can only eat and drink when their environment is one in which they feel safe.

I will return to the subject of the horse's needs in a moment, but for now we need to ask ourselves a question:

> If we are truly to take responsibility for our horses and we are truly committed to their health and well being, are there ways we can provide this type of environment or at least a close approximation to it?

It was in order to do this that I developed the ideas surrounding the principles of natural horse keeping. If a horse is kept within those principles, it has to be kept in a way that approximates a natural life, but I realize that some readers will still be reluctant to give up the stables, the horseshoes, blankets, regular mealtimes and all that goes with that type of management. After all, it is so rewarding and we need to understand why something so rewarding to us is so alien to the nature of the horse.

Take a look at the diagram below, it is graphical illustration of the typical life of a predator:

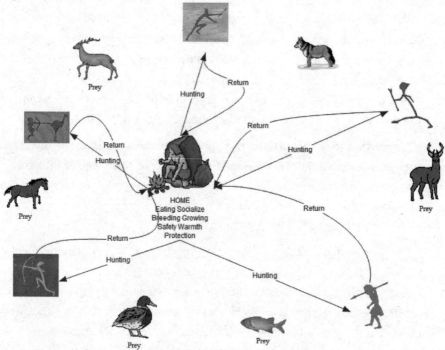

Notice how life is centered around a den or home area and most of the hunter's activities are about going out from this area and returning to it. **Life here is centered around the home.** Along with the importance of eating and socializing, sexual behavior and most important of all, the home is the center of emotional security. It is where humans feel protected, warm, and safe.

Think about almost any terrestrial predator you like, and think about the state they are in when they are born, usually naked, dependent on mother, hairless, frequently blind and deaf, a situation that only changes slowly, usually over a period of weeks or months. Animals like this need the protection of a den or cave to survive this time of total vulnerability. Now think about nearly every prey animal, for instance, deer, cattle, antelope and horses, what state are they in when they are born; are they blind and hairless? No! They are born ready to get up and run. They are up on their feet and moving within a few hours. They start to nibble at grass and after only a few days, they cannot afford to be vulnerable. They are prey animals from the moment they are born.

This diagram shows why the "home" is so important to us and to any predator, this is what is at the center of our comfort zone. This is why we feel so safe when we are in our inner sanctum and why it is the place we feel compelled to seek out when we feel vulnerable or sick. And...

This is why anthropomorphic people assume this is where the horse will feel the same emotions. Unfortunately, this is not the case, because when we trap a horse in a "cave" we are trapping it at the center of *our* world! For a horse to feel emotionally at ease in this environment it would have to deny its very nature as a prey animal.

Note: If you think this diagram is OK for cavemen but doesn't apply to us, just replace hunting with *working* and *shopping*! The diagram won't change, only the labels.

Now compare it with the prey animal diagram below:

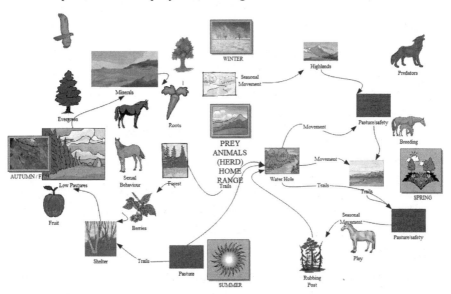

Notice how this diagram lacks a central focal point and is based on traveling, foraging and moving toward things, and searching and finding things when they are needed. Notice how it works perfectly with the seasonal calendar, and how integrated with their environment horses are. Emotionally, there is another element to this: It is the element of *freedom* and *choice*. This is a life which is focused on *positive reinforcement*. First, a need is identified then satisfied—such as the need to eat or drink. This is also an environment based on learning and knowledge. The greater the level of knowledge acquired collectively by the herd, the greater the level of herd security. The greater the level of emotional reward and reinforcement, the more secure and safe the herd feels. This is an environment that is all about feeling safe, and growing more safe and secure through gathering individual and collective knowledge of resources. In short, this is a prey animal's environment.

Nutritionally rich and nutritionally poor environments

As you can see, predator and prey animals live completely different lives, and because of their basic conflicting natures, they live in ways that are in *complete opposition*. Consequently, they favor environments that are in complete opposition and therefore, see the universe in completely different ways. For example:

- The hunter lives in an environment where food is known about but not obvious. It must be found by careful planning, then stalked, captured and killed before it can be eaten.

- The prey animal lives in an environment where almost everything it can see is potentially edible! Every tree, bush or blade of grass could potentially provide nutrition and energy. Horses are literally surrounded by food. It is this ability to extract energy from almost any form of vegetation that has allowed horses to specialize in one of the most abundant food sources on the planet—plant fiber. Being a fiber digester fits perfectly with their life as a prey and flight animal. By foraging and trickle feeding on fiber, horses are able to be very efficient in extracting energy from very poor food sources, while still retaining the ability to run away from predators. This means they have been able to exploit environments that are what I call, "nutritionally poor environments."

Horses also *like to live in an environment that is open and exposed* where they can see for a long distance to detect possible predators. This is why horses don't like enclosed spaces like stables and horse trailers, and this is why your horse will hurry through narrow places or even panic in such situations.

Think about where horses come from. Think of the Arabians who come from open deserts; breeds like the Andalusian or the Lusitano from arid Spain and Portugal; think about the Mustangs, specialists in living in the high rocky mountains of the USA. Think of the pony breeds from northern Eurasia living on tundra, moorlands and cold wetlands. Think about what all these environments have in common.

They are all exposed environments where visibility is high. The majority of the environments are also rather dry, harsh, arid places where vegetation has only short growing periods, rapidly becoming dry, tough and fibrous. Often temperatures vary wildly from the mild to the extreme, both with the climate and the season. This is why horses are traveling, foraging, fiber-digesting, flight animals, and this is the nature of the environment they have evolved to exploit.

Most of the time the vegetation in such environments is based on long fiber and horses have to move and travel constantly to find more food. Horses are able to exploit plant food sources that have very short growing and flowering seasons. Plants that grow rapidly and quickly become fibrous requires a *digestive system highly efficient at extracting energy from a nutritionally poor environment. We* know this because *this is where they choose to live.*

Nutritionally rich environments

Now contrast all that with our predator environment. Successful hunters are those who are very good at finding food. Successful hunters are the ones who survive, pass on their genes and provide "resources" for their families. This notion of what is good or successful carries on to this day. We consider those in our society who are "more successful," "privileged" or "rich" to control a lot of resources. The fundamental difference between rich and poor is not only money (a symbolic representation of resources), but also material things. In other words they own a lot of "stuff." So in the human mind, the richer in resources the environment in which you live, the more "successful" you are as a human being. And, the more "powerful" you are.

- The result of this is that we regard nutritionally-rich environments as highly desirable.

This is fine for humans, but as we now know, humans also have a deadly obsession with anthropomorphism. This is the reason why we feel so rewarded when we shower our horses with luxuries and why we love to "treat" our horses and buy them "stuff." This is why we regard people who do this as generous owners who really care about their animals. This is why we are happy to force feed horses cereals and molasses but regard feeding low grade fibrous feeds like hay or straw as somehow depriving our horse. This is why it feels so good to us to protect them with clothing and luxury accommodation because we think if we provide them with every resource they could ever need as a human, they should be happy, *and this is why we cannot understand when they are not.*

These things are among the first we must understand about the horse as a herd animal when we consider how it fits into the environment. But now let's return to look at the needs of the horse both as an individual and then the needs of the herd in more detail:

Individual needs: personal safety

The horse has a basic desire to survive, and in order to survive as a prey animal, it must be able to detect and react to threats. That means, for its own safety, it must be able to use any of its self-defense strategies, such as flight or fight at any time in its life. This is why horses choose to live on open ground but it is also why they choose to live in herds. As a herd animal, a horse must be able to rely on the presence of other horses to alert it to danger. This is the first and most fundamental need of a horse. A horse must live with other horses.

Detection and movement

Detection and movement working together as one is usually the direct result of the other. *The horse must be able to move at all times*, everything about a horse is designed by evolution to allow it to detect danger and react by movement.

- The horse has the largest eyes in relation to its body of any land mammal. Its eyes are set on each side of its head so that even when grazing at ground level it can see all around it.

- The horse's eyes give it a 360-degree field of vision; they operate using peripheral vision rather than the focused eyes of a hunter.

- The horse has direction finding ears that detect sounds and pinpoint their location this includes the use of the body to act as a sounding board that reflects and magnifies aural information.

- The horse moves with maximum efficiency on a single-toed hoof.

- The horse has large lungs, wide nostrils and a large, powerful heart, so that oxygen can be rapidly carried to the muscles of movement and allow maximum speed for the avoidance of a threat.

- So, to a horse: Detection + Movement = Safety.

Movement for safety is therefore the second most fundamental need of the horse and as you can see, *the second need of the horse is dependent on the first.*

Grazing and drinking

The third need of the horse is the ability to eat and drink in order to maintain its bodily health. Once again, this need is dependent on the first two needs. It would be very unwise for a flight animal like a horse to carry a stomach full of food around with it, so horses have evolved as "trickle" feeders, constantly grazing and moving. Horses will spend up to 16 out of 24 hours a day foraging and eating. It is this process of movement and grazing that causes a horse to cover so much distance every day. At least once a day the horse must also visit a source of water to drink; its survival and health depend on this. Without the freedom of movement a horse cannot move onto fresh pasture or find the herbs and wild plants it needs to self-medicate and maintain its health.

> You may know of horses that have been taken to a local show for the day and even though food and water were provided, the horse did not eat or drink until it returned home, this was because the horse did not feel safe and could not react to that feeling by avoiding it.

Rest and sleep

Another need of the horse that is essential for its well being is the ability to sleep, once again this need is dependent on the preceding needs.

- Horses actually only **truly** sleep for about 20-40 minutes per 24-hour period.

This type of sleep is called R.E.M. (rapid eye movement) and is also known as paradoxical sleep (PS). It is a very particular type of sleep during which it is believed the brain dreams and the muscles relax fully. Dog owners are familiar with REM sleep. It is the sleep accompanied by twitching and "running" movements with the feet. The dog will whimper, bark or appear to make drinking and swallowing movements in its throat. Horses show the same symptoms as dogs, they will lie down and the feet will move rapidly. They will let out short whinnies and will twitch actively. The reason that R.E.M. sleep is so short is that *it is always done while lying down* and this is a big risk for a prey animal. Because REM sleep involves complete relaxation of the muscles, the horse must lie down to achieve it.

REM sleep also happens in humans every night. In experiments, subjects deprived of this type of sleep can develop severe behavioral and sleep problems. Human doctors will always look for abnormal or disturbed sleep patterns as an indicator of stress, depression and other mental illness.

In horses there is a condition known as *Equine Sleep Disorder.* In this condition horses will literally begin to "fall" asleep while standing up and will even partially collapse. The reason for this condition is that the basic needs of the horse are not being met, in other words, *the horse does not feel safe enough to lie down and enter REM sleep.* The causes of this condition are closely linked with prolonged entrapment in a stable. I have successfully treated this condition in one of my horses. The solution was to return the horse to a herd environment so it can feel safe enough to lie down and sleep fully. This is a direct application of the principle of changing the environment, not the horse.

Other sleeping periods of the horse's day are spent dozing and resting. Once again these needs are fundamental to the well being and health of the horse. There is a common idea that horses do not actually need to lie down to sleep because they have a mechanism in their legs that helps them stand up and lock their legs in a standing position. While this is partially true, the type of sleep associated with this position is called slow wave sleep (SWS) and is similar to dozing. It is not REM sleep. The fact that horses with ESD will literally collapse to their knees shows that horses cannot remain standing during the REM period. A horse needs both types of sleep to be healthy.

Body care

Body care of the horse, *by the horse*, is often overlooked and simply not seen as a need, especially by owners who spend hours everyday cleaning, grooming and blanketing their animals. But the fact is, the ability to look after his own body and maintain it, is essential for a healthy horse. Denying the horse the ability to do this because it is simply inconvenient for the human, has serious implications for the welfare of the horse. Bodily health is a vital component of mental health. Horses that are denied these activities quickly become sick.

> Sickness is not a pleasant emotional experience for a prey animal, it makes them vulnerable. I'm sure you can work out who predators are liable to select as a easy meal from a herd, the old, the young, and the sick.

Horses have their own body care routines they must be able to engage in as part of their daily routine. These include activities like scratching against objects, trees for preference, rolling in the mud to rid themselves of parasites and excess hair, and to condition their skin (usually to the great annoyance of their owners).

Temperature regulation

There are wider considerations that should be included under body care, one of the most important of which is the ability to *regulate **their own** temperature*. This means horses need to have the freedom to shelter from the elements including not just cold and wet weather, but also excessive heat, sunshine and flies. Shelter, or rather freedom to choose from various shelter opportunities within the environment, is a vital consideration when designing domestic environments for horses. Horses are perfectly adapted to do this and the natural environment is one of *constantly varying temperatures*. Contrast this with the environment of a house or a cave which is an environment of constant temperature.

Minerals, vitamins and self-medication

Horses naturally seek out minerals and vitamins they need to balance their diet and to self-medicate with plant species if they can. As usual all these ingredients are available within the home range and horses will invest a great deal of time and precious energy in seeking them out. Knowledge of these and other seasonal resources are a great asset to the herd.

Hooves and movement

Horses are creatures of movement and the part of the horse's body that is in lifetime contact with the environment are the hooves. It is the environment that dictates the shape and form of the hoof. It is this shape, sculpted and formed by the environment of the wild horse, that barefoot trimmers try to emulate. To a certain extent the toughness of the hoof is dictated by the components of the diet, so horses that live barefoot need three vital ingredients in order to have healthy feet:

- a natural diet, rich in the right nutrients, vitamins and minerals to help build tough horn
- physical movement and exercise to maintain blood, bone and tendon health
- an environment that shapes and sculpts the hoof through abrasion

In the very broadest sense, we must consider that the ability to care for their own feet and maintain their hooves is an aspect of the horse's body care and personal hygiene.

These are just a few of the physical needs of an individual horse but the horse is, or should be, a member of a herd. We must also consider that the bonds formed between members of a herd are of immense importance to every member, so the horse also has collective needs. The difference is that these needs are primarily *mental* and *emotional*.

Collective needs of the herd: permanence

Once again the basis of this need is safety. Horses need other horses to be both physically and mentally healthy. The important word here is "permanent"—the ability for horses to be with the same group of horses 24/7. In the natural world these bonds are frequently maintained for life, potentially 40 to 50 years. Most horses form relationships based on the notion of families or "harem groups." These bonds are especially strong between *both* parents and their offspring, and a great deal of information about being a successful horse is passed between them. Without these bonds many horses miss out on information that could save their life.

Copying or modeling

Later I will consider how horses learn, but for now it is true to say that in both humans and horses the ability to copy the behavior of those around us as we grow up is one of the most powerful ways of learning many of the vital, complex, social behaviors we use later in life. Some examples might be the way mares pass on the skills of motherhood to their daughters or the ways a stallion might pass on the skills of combat and defense of the herd to his sons. Without these skills, the herd cannot invest in its future success and may die out. A lot of this behavior is learned and practiced by young horses through a series of modeling and "successive approximation" activities or, as we say in plain English, playing.

> When horses are, for whatever reason, reared by humans they miss out on this social learning aspect. These horses often become "imprinted" on humans, effectively relating to humans as their herd mates rather than to other horses. This leads them into showing all kinds of inappropriate behaviors toward humans in the human environment. It also is a big trap for anthropomorphic humans as well, leading to very confused horses and even more confused owners!

Play

It is my observation that males tend to indulge in play type behaviors more than females and the ability to use play behaviors as a method of learning and practicing social behaviors is a vital need for the mental health of a horse. Through playing, both humans and horses achieve something that is beneficial to them, and therefore positively rewarding. There are two types of behavior in play: *copying (or modeling)* and *investigation.* Both are important to positive mental health.

> In the last section of the book I will look at using positive methods, and **only** positive methods, to train horses. Copying/modeling is one such method we will look at in greater detail, but for now we only need to know that it is a positive way of teaching and learning behaviors.

Investigation allows the horse to find out about the world around it and to discover for himself what is safe and what is not. Learning this skill is one of the most important things a horse can ever do. I call this skill a *learning mechanism.* Horses are, for obvious reasons, natural skeptics. They must very quickly learn what is safe and what is not. If they didn't have this ability they would literally end up afraid of their own shadows. This can actually happen especially in answer to unavoidable enforced stress applied over and over again during "training." It results in a state state called sensitization where just about everything is seen as a danger and invokes flight or fight.

The need for play, like all others, is dependent on the need for safety. In the wild a foal that feels safe and happy is usually a curious and playful animal. This feeling of safety and stability comes from its parents, especially a wise mother. Behaviorists say that the foal has a "secure base" from which to explore the world. This means that under the watchful supervision of its mother, the foal can explore and learn (to its great satisfaction) which things in its environment are safe and need not be feared, and which things need to be treated with caution. The ability to voluntarily learn through exploration and play is a vital part of the horse's development and growth throughout its life. A horse that cannot do this lives in a world where it has to cope with continual unknown and therefore frightening things. Because the horse is constantly being presented with new stimuli that are unknown and potentially frightening, the emotional connections are invariably skeptical and thus negative. The horse also becomes reluctant to investigate things that are associated with the negative stimulus and so learns very little about its environment and lacks confidence in interacting with it.

There is a lot of new research being carried out into the emotional effects on foals that are the victim of enforced early weaning—a traditional practice in some types of utility model. There are also considerable implications for the condition known as "separation anxiety" where the horse becomes highly agitated in response to the separation from other horses. As ever this is an example of enforced negative punishment, with the consequent effects on the horse's physical and emotional health.

Territory and exploration

Just as the individual's second most basic need is for movement, so it is the second most basic need for the herd. The herd must move to continually and knowledgeably find food and water and the things its members need to sustain themselves throughout the cycle of the year. There is a popular myth that wild horses are aimless wanderers who move from one place from another only in response to a shortage of food or water. Nothing could be farther from the truth, Horses do wander, but not aimlessly. They wander purposefully in order to avoid encountering shortages in food and water. Horses are always on their way from somewhere, to somewhere. This gives them a sense of positive purpose and allows them to sustain their mental and physical health by finding the things they need to maintain it. We must take this into consideration when we design an environment for the horse because it relates to the principle that horses have a right to live in a stimulating environment.

Wandering aimlessly into the unknown would not be wise for a prey animal. Horses for this reason are creatures of routine—they stick to what they know and what is safe to them. As they continue in this routine, they learn more and more about their environment and it is not unreasonable to assume that this accumulated, safe knowledge is passed down from generation to generation especially through the alpha mares and stallions. When horses wander purposefully they tend to stick to the same routes and pathways that they know link familiar points. Take a look back at the prey animal diagram to see an illustration of this. Indeed you may have seen this with your own horses. You will notice that horses use the same pathways and wear tracks in the paddock that they pass along regularly.

On track

So we can say that for the majority of the time whenever horses move about their home range they do so in a way that is intentionally *"on track."* Hold that thought as it is one of the most important points in the book. Movement *on track* is so important to the herd it becomes the central purpose of their lives. It also is the key to understanding how to create an environment for your horse that meets most, if not all, of the requirements we have looked at so far. We will look at this in greater detail in the next chapter. But first a summary of the points covered in this chapter on the horse's environment.

Summary Chapter 8: The Environment

- Horses live within an area of the environment called the home range.
- Horses are creatures of nutritionally poor environments.
- Humans favor nutritionally rich environments.
- Personal needs of the horse:

- safety
- detection and movement
- grazing and drinking
- rest and sleep
- body care
- temperature regulation
- mineral vitamins and self-medication
- hooves and movement
- Collective needs of the herd:
  - socializing within a permanent herd
  - copying or modeling
  - play
  - territory and exploration
  - life, on track

Chapter 9
What Is a Track System?

Track systems are also known as "paddock paradise" systems. Paddock Paradise is a management system for horses based on allowing the herd constant movement, should they choose to take it, around a continuous, looped track. This system was first proposed by Jamie Jackson in his inspirational book *Paddock Paradise* published in 2006 by Star-Ridge Publishing.

Although the basic idea is deceptively simple, consisting of little more than creating a perimeter track using electric tape, I believe track systems to be possibly one of the most revolutionary ideas in the management of horses for many hundreds (possibly thousands) of years.

In order to justify that statement, let's take a look at some of the many advantages and consider how the needs of the horse discussed in the last chapter are met by this system.

Movement on track

First of all—and I'm sure you are getting the idea—horses are creatures of movement. In the wild this movement is almost constant, with horses traveling as far as 20-30 miles every day of their lives. This is something undertaken by even the youngest foals—foals that must be able to travel with the herd within a few hours of birth. It is this lifestyle of constant movement that keeps wild horses in the peak of physical fitness and it is this movement and the ability to forage over a wide area that allows the horse to live in nutritionally poor environments where they specialize in extracting energy from very low quality, fiber-based food sources. It is this drive to move and travel and the consequent athletic ability that we humans find to be the most useful aspect of the species to exploit to our advantage.

Feeding a fiber-based diet on track

The natural daily feeding pattern of the horse is based on "trickle feeding"—a constant browsing and moving-on behavior—that is the primary daily activity of the herd. A Paddock Paradise or track-based system restores this natural drive to move. Fiber rich food sources, such as hay or haylage are placed at intervals around the track and the horses move from resource to resource, in a similar way to their wild relations. Constant movement gives back to the horse its healthy physique by helping to develop muscles, tendons, bones, healthy circulation and respiration. Ridden horses no longer need to be "warmed up" as they are constantly moving all day, every day.

Socializing on track

The track system allows horses to interact normally with other herd members and share activities such as, grazing, dozing, sleeping, playing, social and even sexual behavior. Certain areas of the track are set aside for this. This returns to them the choice and freedom to behave in a way that is natural and enjoyable and thus emotionally positive and reinforcing. The side-effect of this increased physical behavior is a further increase in physical health.

Self-grooming and self-medicating on track

If circumstances allow, horses can access trees for shade and shelter to control their body temperature, and herbs and other mixed species of plant to self-groom and self-medicate. Once again the effect of allowing horses to behave in this way is one that is positively reinforcing and will result in increased health.

Barefoot horses on track

Track systems were initially conceived for barefoot horses and are especially useful for horses prone to laminitis or weight problems. It is simple to restrict the amount of access to grass at all times. Some owners remove access to grass altogether, especially in springtime. By moving the fencing around the perimeter, it is possible to give a controlled amount of access to mature grass during the autumn. The period over which the grass is grazed can be controlled so that poaching of the ground is eliminated and possible infestation by parasites minimized (without use of chemicals). This fulfills the three requirements of healthy barefoot horses:

- a natural diet, rich in the right nutrients, vitamins and minerals to help build tough hoof-horn, provided on track

- physical movement and exercise to maintain, blood, bone and tendon health

- an environment that shapes and sculpts the hoof through abrasion especially if different surfaces are incorporated into the track (e.g., pea-gravel)

Self-renewing system

Since the primary input into this system is hay or haylage it is nice to have a system that actually creates long-stem fiber, thus saving money. In this sense a track system system is self-renewing every year because it creates some of the resources it needs to function. There is some modest cost to setting up this kind of system but if you offset it against the money saved on brought-in foodstuffs, *the system will quickly pay for itself* and continue to do so for as long as you use it, unlike the stable and paddock arrangement that consumes resources and needs constant maintenance.

Track systems are good for the environment

The track system has a great many advantages for the environment and conservation. The area at the center of the track is left to mature for long periods, creating species-rich traditional grassland, similar to the hay meadows of the past. Traditional hay meadows are one of the most threatened agricultural environments in the world today as they are becoming increasingly rare. When grass species are left to mature in this way, they develop extensive mature root systems that allow them to recover quickly from grazing by horses or other livestock. This is the reason that areas of grass plains throughout the world can support such large numbers of herbivores; much of their reserves are held *beneath* the soil in mature root systems that are able to rapidly recover and put out new growth that quickly becomes mature. The root system locks in a great deal of atmospheric carbon that becomes converted back into plant fiber.

I routinely sow large numbers of wild flower seeds in the spring and I have seen substantial increases in numbers of species of plants and animals over the years that I have been using this system.

Imagine the effect if this system was adopted universally over traditional stable/paddock systems. Thousands of acres of grassland could be returned to traditional long-term pastures **as a by-product of keeping horses**.

Health

I think by now I've made the point that positive environments are intrinsically healthy environments in which to live, and horses that live like this are likely to be not only healthier but happier, easier to train, and even more intelligent because their environment is a stimulating one.

Paddock Paradise or track-based systems are the way of the future. They are simple and relatively cheap to set up on even the smallest acreage, and they provide horses with a total environment based on positive reinforcement, meeting all the natural physical and mental needs a herd requires to live long, healthy lives. Track systems meet all the conditions of the principles of natural horse keeping.

I have used a track system for several years and have seen it work through all seasons. I would never go back to an open field system, especially in the spring and summer. I believe this simple system has so many advantages over conventional management methods, I heartily recommend buying Jamie Jackson's book and getting started.

Now that we have an environment that is suitable for the horse and we understand what horses really need, we need to look at some other areas of comparison between the conventional horse keeping model—whatever that is for you—and the natural horse keeping model. We can also start to develop new ways of riding and training. But first, a summary of the points made in this chapter.

Summary Chapter 9: What Is a Track System?

Track systems are a management system for horses based on allowing the herd constant movement—should they choose to take it—around a continuous, looped track.

- Paddock paradise/track systems compliment the natural movement and feeding behaviors of horses.

- Track systems allow herds of horses to behave in a natural way and socialize with each other.

- Track systems are both interesting and stimulating environments allowing horses to interact with the environment in a positive way, especially with regards to caring for their body naturally by rolling, scratching and mutual grooming.

- Track systems are especially suited to barefoot horses and their need to travel and care for their own feet.

- Track systems are self-renewing and actually produce one of the main inputs into the system—long fiber—which makes them highly efficient environments.

- Track systems present enormous benefits to the global environment and encourage biodiversity of all plant and animal species.

- Placing horses in such environments is a way of maximizing the good health and well-being of horses.

Finally the most important point of all:

- Track systems creates a natural environment for horses to live in, based on **positive reinforcement** where the freedom to behave as horses is an integral part of the their environment.

In the next chapter we will look at one final aspect of keeping horses— training horses in the natural horse keeping model—in ways based on positive reinforcement.

Chapter 10
Control and Communication

In this chapter we will start to look at training a horse. Conventional training is all about **control** of the horse's behavior but I want to consider how we can develop a system based not on control but on **communication**. To understand how this works we need to return to our quadrant diagram:

INCREASE	DECREASE
Reinforce/Reward	Punish
Positive Reinforcement Add something positive NATURAL HORSE KEEPING MODEL: **Feminine** Herd life, movement, choice, long-fiber diet Principles of NHK	**Positive Punishment** Add something negative UTILITY MODEL: **Masculine** Physical tools, history, tradition Practical, efficient
Negative Reinforcement Remove something negative NATURAL HORSEMANSHIP MODEL: **Masculine** Hunting AND Training: goals, stalking, driving, ritual	**Negative Punishment** Remove something positive ANTHROPOMORPHIC MODEL: **Feminine** Housing, clothing, shoeing, diet

COMMUNICATION	CONTROL
Natural Horse Keeping: positive reinforcement training, clicker training, target training, copying/ modeling (mental communication)	**Utility**: bits, bridles, whips, spurs, martingales, chains, blinkers, etc. (physical control)
Natural Horsemanship: round pen, rope halters, sticks and strings (physical communication)	**Anthropomorphic**: stables, blankets, horseshoes, diets (mental control)

As you can see I have added two more boxes to the bottom of the table, "communication" on the left side of the table and "control" on the right. You can see that the right side, dealing with human ideas of utility and anthropomorphism, is associated with control of the horse both mentally and physically. This is because they are closely linked with predator thinking and ideas about hunting, so in the utility model we have lots of physical tools designed to control the natural behavior of the horse, especially the flight response. If you look at horses that are ridden in the traditional English style you will see that their heads are the focus of control. They are constrained by the use of martingales (see below), and their forward momentum is controlled by the application of **pressure** on the mouth and lower jaw through the use of a bit and bridle. This pressure is fairly constantly applied in English riding by the use of reins that are kept in contact with the most sensitive part of the horse's body, the mouth, while the horse is ridden.

Martingales

Martingales are straps, usually connected to the girth, that hold the horse's head in a certain position or at least limit the degree of freedom of movement the horse is able to express; they come in two types, running and standing.

A running martingale has rings that run along the reins. These rings and their connecting straps have two functions: to prevent the horse from raising its head and to ensure the angle on the bit provides constant pressure.

The first function of preventing the horse from raising its head thwarts a natural aspect of the flight reaction in which a horse will elevate its head in order to feel safe, see further and detect predators. If you look at photographs of running or stampeding horses you will see that all of them show this elevated head position. By raising the head in this way the brain is also stimulated to signal the body to produce adrenaline, a hormone that prepares the body for flight. By controlling the elevation of the head, a rider can prevent the body's production of adrenalin, thus reducing the chance of the horse bolting in panic.

The second function of a running martingale is to ensure that the correct angle is maintained on the bit so that it always pulls slightly down and back, maximizing pressure on the horse's lower jaw, and in the case of a linked bit, puts pressure on the roof of the horse's mouth.

Standing martingales are usually nothing more than a single strap connected directly from the girth to the back of the nose band. Standing martingales hold the horse's head rigidly in one position and prevent the horse raising its head at all. Their use is sometimes frowned upon and even considered cruel, but others regard them as an important training tool or a practical and efficient way to prevent the horse displaying undesirable behaviors.

Pressure

The use of the word pressure here is an interesting one. When people talk about using a stronger bit or a harsher bit or talk about riding the horse into the bit, what do you think they mean? Well, what they mean is pain. Pain is what has been used to control the flight reaction of horses for thousands of years. Here is a photograph I like to show my students when I give talks. It shows two bits, similar in appearance, that work in exactly the same way. The only thing separating them is 3,000 years of history. One is a 21st century bit, the other was found on a bronze age archaeological site and is dated at 1300 BC. So much for human technology!

Bronze Age bit
circa 1300 BC Greece

Modern twisted-wire bit
USA

- Another big disadvantage with the use of pressure/pain is that it is another of those words that mean different things to different people. One person's "strong" bit is another person's "normal" bit.

If you remember the coercion test of, "comply with my wishes or else suffer the consequences," you will see that by having a handy way of inflicting pressure—literally at our fingertips—we have a useful way of controlling the horse through the threatened use of positive punishment.

Whips and spurs

I don't propose to go through the whole range of equipment used on horses but the use of whips and spurs shows a different version of physical tools used to control the natural behavior of the horse, whips and spurs are used to drive a horse. They work on the principle of moving the horse away from discomfort towards comfort or at least the evasion of pressure. In this way they are tools used in *driving behaviors*.

Conventional training is based on our hunting instincts

In the chapter on natural horsemanship I said it is based on our hunting instincts. This is also true of conventional training, perhaps even more so. All the common elements are there:

- a goal or idea of what is to be achieved
- practical and efficient ways of achieving the goal
- persistence until the goal succeeds
- control over the horses head and thus direction
- the systematic removal and restriction of the flight and fight reactions
- driving behaviors
- frequently a symbolic final act in the achievement (the horse does what is asked) and a rewarding feeling for the predator

This is how physical tools are used in the utility model. They are all based on tradition, ideas about what works and what doesn't, and what is the most practical and efficient way of achieving that control. This is why there has been so little change for the last 3,000 years. This is the utility model, but what about the anthropomorphic model? How is it used to control horses' natural behavior?

Anthropomorphic tools

The tools of the anthropomorphic model are just as much about control as bits and whips, they are based on the four foundational ideas of:

- diet
- housing
- clothing
- horseshoes

The difference between the two models is that these tools of control are all about mental control. They are enforced environments of negative punishment from which the horse has no escape. You cannot run away from an enforced environment.

Merged training methods

The anthropomorphic model does not have a specific training style associated with it as both the utility and natural horsemanship training methods are now being used. It is common practice to send one's horse away to a trainer to be "broken" (or "gentled") or otherwise trained to meet a specific "level" of training—as marketed by the trainer—in 90 days or less. Trainers have begun to customize their programs, using both utility and natural horsemanship methods as needed to meet their first priority: *the timeframe.* This is how the trainer's degree of success—and reputation—is determined by their clients. Human priorities tend to be *easier, faster, better.* In response to these priorities, a 3-day event has gained popularity over the past several years in the U.S., in which trainers compete to break a colt and ride it through an obstacle course with *the least amount of incident* which defines "success" in this scenario. The event centers around the very limited time each trainer has with a horse and what methodology meets the goal within the limited time. To the extent the trainer can hint at why their method is least stressful (in obviously stressful circumstances) for the horse, he additionally gets the public nod as "humane." The implications for the winning trainer is that his or her name and method gains notoriety as being the "best," capable of delivering the "fastest" success in comparison to the other trainers. Once again, the human agenda is met.

Breeding

Another example of control vs. communication might be most people's attitude to breeding horses—per the utility model. The mare is usually sent to a stud farm where she is serviced in the most practical and efficient way. Once again the natural behavior of the horse is of no consequence because it is irrelevant to its purpose. Virtually all of the natural behavioral interaction between mares and stallions (a huge part of the natural ethogram) is suppressed as it is not relevant.

Note: Of all "working" horses, breeding stallions and mares have the toughest time. **They are the most utility based of all utility model horses**, frequently they exist only **to fulfill a single function**, breeding or drug manufacturing. The treatment of the mares and loss of the foals in the process at PMU farms is an example of how humans can overlook an otherwise unconscionable use of horses if it meets a human agenda or has a monetary reward associated with it.

Additionally, when mares are inseminated using artificial methods there is a suppression of the natural and instinctive behaviors of the horse, but as it provides a total removal of the "inconvenience" of stallion behavior, it is regarded as ideal—ideal for the human.

So many horses get the worst of both models—spending long hours in a stable—only to be ridden or trained for a brief time, after which they are returned to the stable. Given the effects on their health of enforced negative punishment and the coercive nature of conventional training it is no wonder horses "learn to be helpless," suffering ever increasing levels of disease and ultimately dying younger.

Communication

Moving on to something more positive: What about training based on communication? The only way of achieving this is to use a different behavioral law: positive reinforcement.

The fundamentals of positive reinforcement training (PRT)

There are several types of positive reinforcement training, the most well-known of which is clicker training. Many people will tell you that it only takes a few minutes to learn how to positively train a horse, but that it will take you years to understand why it works. Although this might be partially true, I think it is more accurate to say it will take you years to realize the potential of what you have. The theory side of it is very straightforward, you only need to understand three things:

- classical conditioning
- operant conditioning
- the difference between a treat and a reward

The first two might sound a little daunting but actually they are really simple to understand. For instance the word "conditioning" is really just a scientific way of saying *learning*.

Classical conditioning

The key to understanding whether a behavior is classically conditioned or not, is the word *"predicts."* When a behavior is classically conditioned, it simply means the animal learns that two or more events are linked together—the event predicts something will happen. Let me use my dogs as an example:

I keep my dogs' leashes hanging in the kitchen cupboard. When the dogs see me open the door and take down the leashes they know it's time for a walk. This creates a change in their behavior. Previously they have been curled up fast asleep but now, they become excited and jump around in anticipation of the walk (or "hunt" as they would see it—I also respect my dogs as dogs). This is a typical classically conditioned response where one event predicts another that, in this case, is emotionally rewarding.

Operant conditioning

Some dogs are so clever that when they consider it time for a walk, they will go and find their leash and bring it to their owner. This is called "operant conditioned behavior," which means:

- the subject takes a specific action in order to **make** something happen.

Note: The odd word "operant" refers to the subject. If for example you were training your horse, you would be the operator and the horse would be the operant. In this case, behavior becomes "operant" when the horse takes some action to make an event occur.

When we train our horse, we should always be looking for ways to get our horse to learn through operant behavior. In this way the horse is learning right along with us and is getting rewarded, also along with us. It is about teaching the horse to look for the right answer so we can reward it, then getting the horse to want to do that thing again because it was emotionally rewarding. Speaking of rewards...

The difference between a treat and a reward

This is one of the most commonly misunderstood ideas around any kind of positive reinforcement, and this is why we clearly need to understand the three points above. Classical conditioning and operant conditioning are not good or bad in themselves. It is the emotions they lead to that are important. This is what sometimes confuses people about conditioning (learning). They don't understand that the emotions the events lead to are more important than the physical events themselves. To put it another way, the behavior is a side effect of the emotions. Nothing illustrates this better than the confusion found around the ideas of treats and rewards. We looked at them before in the section called trick or treats, but here is a quick recap:

- **Treats are not helpful—at all**. I never treat my horses but I do reward them a lot.

- The reason treats are not helpful is that while treats may or may not induce pleasant emotions in the horse, the fact is *it doesn't matter,* because *treats reward the human, not the horse.*

- Treating our horse is a way of giving us *instant good feelings about ourselves.* Normally this is with food but where it gets really strange is when humans extend this idea to horses becoming the owners of material possessions!

Stuff!

Anthropomorphic people buy "stuff" for their horses at such a rate and consistency that it makes a bystander wonder if they believe it actually matters to the horse to have personal belongings. The point is however, people get such pleasure from providing these items—and perhaps from shopping for them—that they want to repeat the experience, creating positive reinforcement for the human.

- Any emotions the horse might possibly have regarding the use of the items are not only ignored, they specifically don't matter.

- The possibility a human might succeed in buying some measure of her horse's affection with "stuff" remains a subconscious incentive.

Have you ever gone to put a blanket on your horse—ignoring the horse's protests—because you believe you know best and are doing your horse a favor?

Rewards

A reward is a specific event in a horse's life intended to get a repeat of a behavior.

You have probably realized that repeating behavior is reinforced behavior and the best way to reinforce a behavior is to make it positive so that it *leads to positive emotions.* Once again it is the emotions we are after, not the physical behavior or material result, although we usually get that as well. This is all part of the positive fallout associated with positive reinforcement training.

- Positive reinforcement training through the use of rewards gives us a direct line to our horse's emotions.

Positive reinforcement is not a system

Unlike systems such as natural horsemanship, positive reinforcement is not a system, it is a "mechanism"—a process that can be repeated *indefinitely* to build positive emotions in your horse and in you. Because we are thinking in terms of a mechanism, the horse never adapts to the mechanism; the mechanism always adapts to the horse. For example, certain horses are really good at moving their feet; they are athletic and like to move around. This gives us all kinds of behaviors that we can reward and use. Other horses are less athletic but love to think things out, they enjoy puzzling over something and getting the answer, this also gives us lots of behaviors that we can reward but because of the positive side effects of the mechanism, the "smart" horse will become more athletic and the athletic horse will get smarter as part of their attempts to find out what is rewarded. So the mechanism constantly adapts and develops the horse; the horse never has to adapt to the system.

Right behaviors and "wrong" behaviors

- With positive reinforcement training we are always looking to reward the right thing. We **never** look to correct the wrong thing.

You might remember the section on the utility model where I mentioned that traditional teachers base their teaching on correction. This means that the teacher is looking for the "wrong" answer so they can correct it.

- Correction by the way, is positive punishment and horses don't like it any more than children or husbands!

By basing training on correction, the teacher actually **needs** the horse to do "wrong things" so that they can teach something! Perhaps you experienced something similar at school?

In positive reinforcement training *there are no wrong answers*. In fact, both student and teacher are so focused on the right answer that the worst consequence of a wrong answer is that nothing happens! I actually take wrong answers a step further and make them into a positive, by letting the horse know that it just earned the opportunity of a "free go!" My horses love this. So remember:

- We only reward the "right" answer.
- There are no "wrong" answers just neutral responses.
- The "wrong" response always earns a "free go."

Extinction

Some people are a bit puzzled by this ignoring of the wrong answer, after all it's not something we got a lot of in our own education, so it seems a bit odd to us. But the reason we are ignoring the wrong behavior is that we want it to go into "extinction," i.e., to disappear. When we say the behavior is not rewarded, we mean it is not emotionally rewarded and when behavior is not rewarded in this way it no longer serves a purpose, so the subject automatically switches to finding a behavior that is rewarded. The other side of this is that if you do accidentally reward an emotional response you don't want, you can end up on the wrong track, but PRT is very forgiving and now you know how to undo the damage, just ignore it (a neutral response) and the subject will automatically switch to the right track.

Natural horsemanship tools

On the left side of the table we have natural horsemanship and natural horse keeping. There are physical and mental "tools" used on this side and for the most part, they are (usually) used for communication rather than to control the horse's behavior. This is why I say that natural horsemanship is a great step forward in the thinking of humans. Natural horsemanship moves the emphasis from predator thinking—what the human wants—toward prey animal thinking—what the horse wants. Typical natural horsemanship tools include:

- rope halter
- fiberglass stick similar to an elongated riding crop
- horseman's string—a six-foot length of rope with many useful applications
- long lead at least 12 feet in length
- round pen

These are the basic tools that are generally regarded as useful in applying gentler means of communication than conventional tools and are *ideally* never used with the intention of controlling the horse through pain even though they do have many applications where they are used with the intention of threat. This is because a lot of natural horsemanship is based on the idea of increasing and releasing pressure (negative reinforcement). Another factor to consider is that humans are tool-using predators which leaves how these tools are used completely up to humans using them—determined by their intuition, intellect, and emotional control. As a result these tools can potentially be used both painfully and aggressively. When this happens we have an example of the horse being forced to adapt to the system and it is these tools that are used to do it.

Usually a natural horsemanship exercise is described in terms of a desired physical outcome, although the process used to achieve it is highly subjective and up to the interpretation of the student. For example, the instructions might say, "don't use more pressure than phase 3," but as I've pointed out before, one person's phase 3 could be another person's phase 10! This is further compounded by a lot of natural horsemanship being taught as distance-learning courses, leaving the interpretation completely up to the human student without necessarily understanding *how* to interpret the instructions. Not surprisingly, the usual result is confusion.

Positive reinforcement tools

In positive reinforcement training, there are very few tools. When tools are used they are used more as "props" to facilitate the training. For example, I take the horseman's string used in natural horsemanship and apply it as a neck strap, then reward the horse for responding to a stimulus around the neck. I might use the fiberglass stick and have the horse follow it as a target. The most obvious tool used in PRT is the use of a *bridging signal* usually in the form of a clicker, and of course, a bag of food rewards. That is about it. I will explain clearly what I mean by a bridging signal in a moment.

Optional tools in natural horse keeping

There are some optional tools that can be used with positive reinforcement training. These are all tools *that communicate a cue to the horse that can be rewarded*, particularly useful ones are bitless bridles such as the Dr. Cook cross-under bitless bridle. This type of bridle works perfectly with positive reinforcement because no discomfort is caused to the horse, therefore there is no element of threat. This type of bridle also works really well with the idea of refinement (see below) and so quickly becomes a very subtle tool indeed.

Note: The term "cue" here is simply a stimulus that at first, asks for a behavior and after a few repetitions will come to predict that behavior.

Treeless saddles

Another optional tool I use is a treeless saddle. Traditional saddles built on a wooden frame or "tree" are yet another idea descended from the Victorian cavalry. The conventional English general purpose saddle was developed from the light British cavalry saddle. This is why it is used so often in equestrian sports, most of which are also derived from army competitions. The problem with traditional saddles is that their use is based on the idea that they should be fitted to the horse and most of them are not. It is doubtful that even when they are, they are flexible enough to take into account the change in shape of a horse's back as it moves in trot or canter. If you look at the scar tissue on the backs of many horses, this would seem to be the case. Treeless saddles do not have this problem as the better ones change shape with the horse's back. Additionally, pads for their use are designed with a gap in the middle to keep weight off the horse's spine.

If we take the idea of control versus communication we can see that a conventional saddle that causes any discomfort or pain at all will have the potential to be used to control the horse's behavior through the use of threat, i.e., coercion. The horse will do what it needs to, to try to remove the threat through avoidance or even violence.

My favorite saddle is actually little more than a bareback pad. It is treeless and had some fiberglass reinforcements to create a pommel and cantle but I removed them so it is now a pad that fits all my horses and me very well.

Training areas

When I work with horses I like to work within the herd so I don't catch, isolate or trap the horse. I try to always work in their home range. Normally this is not a problem but occasionally inexperienced horses see the presence of a food resource and want to get in on the action, which can become dangerous and distracting. The solution here is to construct a small temporary "play pen" with a few plastic fencing stakes and some tape. The herd readily accepts this and when other horses realize it is not their turn for some reinforcement, they return to grazing after only a minute or so (extinction again).

Clicker training is remembered

When I first started clicker training, I ran into this problem with two of my horses, so I constructed a play pen which solved the problem. This was late in the year and as I was new to this approach I didn't bother to train them during the winter. The following spring I decided to try again and so began to put in the stakes for the pen once more. While I was doing this **the two horses came and stood in the center of the pen area and began offering me behaviors!** They started deliberately moving backwards, forwards and sideways as we had been doing several months before. It was at this point I started to realize how powerful this type of training was. In clicker training terms, the pen area had become classically conditioned with the positive emotions, so that my constructing the pen predicted a clicker training session. The act of offering behaviors is an advanced form of operant conditioning where the horses were trying to work out what would get a click and thus reward.

Increasing pressures versus refinement

As both natural horse keeping and natural horsemanship appear on the same side of the table, both tend to be based on communication rather than control. You might be wondering how the two laws compare. One of the most important differences I have found is in the use of *phases of pressure* used in natural horsemanship and the automatic *process of refinement* that is a feature of positive reinforcement training.

In almost all natural horsemanship systems the idea of increasing phases of pressure is used. One way the Parelli system describes these phases is quite useful. The four phases of pressure are defined as:

- phase one, touch the hair
- phase two, touch the skin
- phase three, touch the muscle
- phase four, touch the bone

As you can see we have an increasing use of pressure here, but that pressure is quickly released when the horse performs the behavior. This is the reward-through-relief element of negative reinforcement, which is why it appears on the left side of the table. In fairness, *most* horses learn to respond quickly to pressure and as long as the principle is applied consistently, it is seldom necessary for the trainer to go further than phase two. We also have the use of coercion—comply with my wishes or else—plus all the rules of coercion. Coercion will always increase, and if we have a use of pressure that is subjective in its application by different people, there is always a danger that what is one person's phase two could be another person's phase four!

It is for these reasons that I do not use negative reinforcement, it is a real weakness at the heart of the system and even some of the most experienced natural horsemen in the world occasionally fall prey to their own instincts. There have been one or two spectacular examples of this posted to the internet which are particularly embarrassing for the trainers involved.

Four phases of positive reinforcement (refinement)

In positive reinforcement training we also use a "phase one." It is always a starting point but the automatic consequence of operant conditioning is that the horse enthusiastically wants to repeat the behavior and is already looking for the cue to earn the click, so instead of moving up to phase two, we move *down* to phase three-quarters, in other words in the opposite direction! The four phases of positive reinforcement are:

- phase one
- phase three-quarters
- phase one-half
- phase one-quarter
- phase zero—total trust

Yes, there is a phase zero, it is that magical connection between horse and trainer that to an outside observer looks like telepathy. This is the goal of clicker training and this is when the "bridge of trust" is completed. Further work on the bridge serves only to strengthen it, (see next chapter for more on this idea). An example of phase zero might be a behavior you trained by touching the horse by putting your hand on his nose and getting him to take a step backwards. You might then refine this until the horse steps backwards at just a hand signal, this is phase zero. The exciting thing is that this phase zero can now become the new phase one and you could further refine this until your horse steps backwards at the twitch of a finger or the raising of an eyebrow! The reason this works is because the horse is actively looking to put in effort to get the reward, so the horse is highly motivated to *make more effort.*

Only positive reinforcement works in this way while in conventional training or natural horsemanship, each new exercise has to be learned as a separate item requiring moving up through the phases in order to teach it. The danger here is that the horse interprets this as a situation in which it can never win. Each time you increase pressure you will get a horse that is working out what is the *minimal effort* it must make to evade the pressure. It has no incentive to do anything else. If you think about the way an alpha horse uses negative reinforcement it is with the intention of getting another horse to comply with the alpha's wishes. In other words, the end result of using negative reinforcement *must be* compliance.

Whether you use negative or positive laws, learning will always take place, That is because we are dealing with universal laws—in this case, the laws of learning.

The four laws of learning

When humans or horses learn anything we tend to pass through four distinct phases. Because these phases are the same for all living things—at least most animals—we know that we are dealing with universal laws. The four stages are:

- linking
- repeating
- generalizing
- maintaining

The first law: linking

When we come across new information and experiences, our brains store the information as a memory by:

- linking new information to something we already know

This means we cannot learn anything new in isolation; we have to store it in this way by linking it to *something*. Our brains will do this whether we like it or not, so the trick is to make sure it becomes linked to the right bit of existing information. It is the same for horses. We saw this in the section on classical conditioning where two ideas become linked together. However, it is also possible for many ideas to become linked to the same information in a way that predicts a behavior or event. I used the example of my dogs seeing me take the leashes from the kitchen cabinet and this predicted it was time for a walk, but of course, there were many other ideas or "cues" linked to my behavior, such as the time of day, picking up my keys or putting on my coat. Additionally, one of the most powerful ideas of all, it was linked to a daily routine or repetition.

The second law: repeating

We have two types of memory: short term and long term. Our short-term memory allows us to deal with our everyday lives, making sense of the information we receive through our senses. In order for us to retain information however, we must repeat the information a few times. This is how learning moves from our short term to long-term memory. The more it is repeated, the more thoroughly the lesson is learned. If you try to memorize something, you realize that just reading it through or hearing it once is not enough. You have to repeat it several times before you can remember it accurately. When you teach a new behavior to a horse you will have to repeat it several times to make sure the horse has gotten it.

- A key point here is that experiences repeated along with emotion are learned very quickly and remembered very readily.

Unfortunately this also works against us when negative emotions are involved. This is why experiences that are associated with unpleasant emotions such as a visit from the vet, are quickly and deeply learned.

On the plus side, horses are very quick learners, because they are prey animals, (the slow learners don't survive very long). You will find that if you can teach a horse something it associates with positive emotions, such as excitement, curiosity, fun or any other generally good feelings, it will be remembered rapidly and the horse will be eager to repeat it. This is why we should always work on building that bridge of trust; the horse will associate what we do with good decisions that lead to positive feelings, and the horse will feel rewarded because it has made a good choice.

The third law: generalizing

Because the brain links information to things we already know, horses and humans soon realize that things they have learned have other applications. For example, as children we learn to read and soon we realize that this skill has all kinds of other applications throughout our life, well beyond the classroom. Horses are the same; you might teach a horse to touch its shoulder to your hand; in order to do this the horse must make a small movement sideways to make the contact. This is the beginning of a whole group of behaviors that involve sideways movement, and they can all be developed from this small beginning. This exercise could be developed in various ways, for instance, it allows you to place a horse in any position around you, it is the beginning of lateral movements from the saddle, it is how you can teach a horse to move sideways towards a gate and so on. This is a principle used a great deal in clicker training and it is called *shaping*, where you take a small, even accidental behavior, and reward it. From this you can develop a whole range of behaviors moving from the most basic to the extremely advanced.

If you compare this with the section above that dealt with refining cues instead of increasing pressure, you will see that by working with positive reinforcement you can get more and more for less and less. Or to put it another way, you make less and less effort (minimal effort) as the horse starts making more and more effort (maximum effort).

Another principle involving both linking and generalizing is *chaining* behaviors, where you develop a sequence of small behaviors that you teach separately, then link them together into one large sequence of behaviors.

- I sometimes think positive reinforcement training works so well because it works in a way that mimics functions of the brain. Physical exercises become linked and added upon one another in the same way mental ideas and learning are linked and added upon one another.

The fourth law: maintaining

After a behavior has been thoroughly learned, it is still necessary to revisit it from time to time in order for it to be refreshed. This stage is often overlooked. For example, take a subject you studied intensively in school then never revisited. Did you remember it a year later? If we do this in positive reinforcement training, we can renew the emotion as well, because the horse will get a pleasant surprise that something it learned to do before still gets an occasional reward. If we don't do the maintaining stage, just as with our own learning, we will find the memory begins to fade.

More techniques

These are the four laws of learning. They are the four stages that humans and horses go through when they learn anything. I have mentioned shaping and chaining behaviors as important terms so here is some instant repetition—law #3:

Shaping: the ability to take one small (sometimes accidental) behavior and develop it; this is part of the third law of learning—generalizing. For example, we might teach a horse to go backwards from a cue applied to its nose. Teaching a horse to back up is the starting point for all kinds of behaviors related to the halt and collection. We will refine this, to have the horse back from a hand signal (phase zero). We might then develop this so that the horse backs up when they feel a cue from a neck strap, or we might have the horse copy our body language and do a halt and back up, from this we could teach the horse to do half-halts from the ground, thus developing collection. We could then transfer this to a response from the saddle and so on.

Chaining behaviors: learning small component parts of a behavior and linking them together into a larger behavior. In a similar way to shaping, we follow the idea of developing behaviors, and each time we do this we get more behaviors for less reward. When a behavior becomes learned it no longer needs to be rewarded every time. This is a very powerful principle, called variable reinforcement.

Variable reinforcement

I once worked behind the bar in a pub and every day I watched people gambling on a slot machine. I knew that in some cases this money was their grocery money for the week— money they could not afford to spend—yet every person was convinced the machine was going to make a jackpot payment any moment. This is powerful, yet pure emotional thinking. Logically, everyone knows these machines are geared always to make a profit for the owner of the machine, yet that doesn't matter. Each gambler is emotionally convinced he or she will be the one who has the luck to be the big winner. They "know" this because *the machine keeps paying out just enough small prizes to keep them interested.* Variable reinforcement is one of the most powerful aspects of the laws of behavior. It is actually the sliding scale between positive reinforcement and negative punishment, and in the human world this is where we find people who have become *addicted* to this behavior. The key to understanding is the pleasurable experience of surprise, so it is the not knowing if you will be lucky this time that actually leads to the thrill of the experience. This is a universal law, so it also works on horses but don't worry we are not going to end up with a horse that is addicted to being trained—even though that might not be such a bad thing! Let's explore how to apply this powerful principle.

When a horse learns a behavior and gets used to receiving a reward every time it performs the behavior, we don't need to keep rewarding the behavior at a one-to-one ratio. We can start asking for the horse to try harder and perhaps repeat the behavior two or three times for one reward. Because the horse is working harder for the same reward we can gradually extend this until the horse only gets an occasional or variable reward. The horse never knows when this behavior will earn a surprise reward and instead of being disappointed by having to work harder, will actively be excited by the process— because it is fun! In this way we actually start to "fade" the clicker out of the process and can move onto other more exciting exercises based on what the horse already knows. This is the shaping and linking process in action. Variable reinforcement also takes the horse to the fourth law of learning—maintaining. In the next chapter I will look at combining all this information and building a relationship based on communication with your horse.

Summary Chapter 10: Control and Communication

- In the utility model tools and training are all about controlling the natural behavior of the horse.

- In the anthropomorphic model material things and "stuff" are often used to buy the horse's affection.

- Conventional training is based on hunting.

- Natural horsemanship is based on communicating with the horse but uses "phases of pressure" that rely heavily on the knowledge, timing, feel and instincts of the human trainer.

- Positive reinforcement training is based on communication through refinement of pressure and is easier for people who are new to horses to learn.

- Positive reinforcement is based on:
  - classical conditioning
  - operant conditioning
  - knowing the difference between a treat and a reward

- The four universal laws of learning:
  - linking
  - repeating
  - generalizing
  - maintaining

- Clicker training also includes techniques of refinement such as shaping and chaining behaviors.

- Positive reinforcement is a training mechanism—not a system.

- In PRT there is no such thing as a wrong answer, just a neutral "free go" for another attempt.

Chapter 11
Positive Reinforcement Training and Relationships

In this chapter I want to pull together all the ideas I have talked about regarding training your horse and show you how they can be used to build a new and exciting relationship based on positive reinforcement.

In the chapter on the natural horsemanship model, I introduced the idea of a system and I looked at how systems force individuals to adapt to their rules and regulations and how the students that are successful products of these systems are the individuals who adapted most readily to the rules of the system. I also looked at how these systems were highly *inefficient* because they consumed large numbers of resources in terms of time effort and money yet produced large numbers of 'drop-outs', in terms of individuals who failed to adapt to the system. You might have realized that in looking at systems in this way there are certain common familiar themes. The system says:

- Comply with my wishes or else suffer the consequences.

- Systems are enclosed and enforced environments.

- There is a lot of escape through flight (truancy/drop out).

- There is a lot of resistance to the rules of the system through fight (disruption).

- Many student horses adopt an approach of compliance in which they make minimum effort to "tough it out" until the system lets them go.

- Student horses will always make the minimal effort as they have no incentive to do anything more.

All this means we are dealing with systems based on the coercive laws of negative reinforcement, positive punishment and negative punishment. I gave the example of the education system with which we are all so familiar. However, as we have now used up the three coercive laws, we are left with positive reinforcement and that is never based on punishing the wrong thing but on rewarding the right thing.

- Systems force individuals to adapt to the rules, but PRT works the other way around, *adapting to **any** individual.*

- PRT is therefore a process that is open to all, independent of an individual's background, ability, experience.

- PRT is **highly efficient**, because it is inherently rewarding; drop-out rates are minimal and successful outputs are maximized. After all, why would horse or human want to evade a process they found rewarding?

- PRT is a process that works with only minimal inputs because the willing efforts of those being trained make success an *automatic* outcome of the process.

- Because positive reinforcement is a law, it means PRT works on all living things and is therefore not specific to humans.

- PRT does not impose requirements, rules or regulations on the student as happens within a system.

- PRT takes the individual attributes of the student into consideration and develops and enhances individual abilities they already have.

- The student therefore strengthens weaker areas as a consequence (positive fall-out).

- Positive reinforcement is inherently rewarding for both teacher and student because both parties get what they want.

- Students learn rapidly because they are in control of their own learning and always working toward something they desire—wanting to progress.

- Students will always make the extra effort because they have every incentive to do so—the opposite of compliance.

- Because lessons learned are both intellectually and emotionally rewarding, they are remembered with enthusiasm—usually for life.

- Positive emotions are powerful aids to memory and learning.

I believe positive reinforcement and training methods based on its principles, are the next stage in the evolution of the long relationship between horses and humans. Here are the reasons why I make this claim:

We have had millennia of historical and traditional training based on what was *practical* and *efficient*—teaching that was usually taught to the horse by *correction* and the *threat* of consequences. We have begun to move in the right direction with natural horsemanship techniques that take an interpretation of *some* of the natural behaviors of the horse but still use enforced negative reinforcement and the inevitable threat of positive punishment.

Because we no longer need horses to enable us to survive, for the first time in history we have the luxury of allowing ourselves to see our horse for the wonderful animal he really is. By coming to understand the horse as a horse, we will also learn more about ourselves as human beings. I think this is the the biggest reason of all to adopt positive reinforcement methods because of the positive changes *it will make in us*. For example, as we work with our horses and establish more trust with them, we will build their confidence. That in turn, will build *our* confidence, so not only does our horse get better, more trusting, more relaxed and more confident when it is around us, the same thing happens to us when we are around the horse! This is just one of the hundreds of positive spin-offs that we discover as we change our thinking through positive reinforcement training.

The horse is a prey animal and we are predators resulting in the fact that what we want to achieve is usually at odds with what the horse wants to achieve. As the horse is programmed by nature to instinctively do the opposite of what the predator desires, any kind of relationship we build through our management and training of the horse must be one of bridge-building between our opposite natures.

Building the bridge of trust

Nothing positive can be built into a relationship between a prey animal and a predator that is not built on trust.

- In other words, everything we do in management and training of our horse should be with the deliberate aim of building trust between us.

If a horse comes to trust another horse, it means it trusts that horse's *choices* and *decisions*. This is a great example of why some horses become "alphas" in a herd. It is because the individuals that make up the herd trust their choices and thus their decisions.

If you are a prey animal, perhaps the most important choice you make in your life— literally a matter of life and death—is whose decisions do you trust?

So the next question we might ask is:

- What makes us believe the decisions we trust are the right ones?

The answer is a simple one:

- Because those decisions always lead to "good feelings."

As we've seen, the most basic good feeling for the horse is safety. Horses will tend to trust horses (and humans) *that consistently make choices and decisions that reinforce emotional safety.*

If you contrast that with conventional human training, much of our efforts are about *challenging* the horse and *taking away the feeling of safety.*

So to put all that together, we can say that when a horse trusts another creature, it is because he trusts their *emotions.*

This is the key to understanding horse training. It has nothing to do with goals, releasing pressure or correction, it has everything to do with building trust through decisions that lead to good feelings for the horse.

There is one other consequence of training and managing a horse in such a way that it builds trust, and that is a positive side effect much sought after by human beings when they deal with horses—respect.

Respect

Respect is another of those words like "dominance" or discipline that mean different things to different people. Some people who are close to their predator instincts often carry a "control" tool such as a whip with them at all times when they are around horses. I have known people like this. They believe it gives them authority with the horses and means the horses must "respect" them. This is nonsense. The reactions they see when they are around horses are based on fear, not respect.

I once knew someone who would always enter a herd carrying a whip. However, when she came to visit me, she went out to meet my herd without a whip. I was happily talking away with my usual enthusiasm, when I realized something. This person was pale and breathing hard and was actually having a panic attack, because despite a lifetime of being around horses she was actually deeply afraid of them. Before you feel too sorry for this lady, I should also tell you this person was very physically aggressive in her dealings with horses and despite claiming to "love" her animals, was utterly ruthless in the way she dealt with them and had no qualms about disposing of them if they could no longer serve her purpose.

If you trust someone to make decisions that keep you safe and lead you to good emotional feelings, then it is very likely that you will come to feel comfortable with that person. Respecting their choices and actions in this way is the only foundation of *real* respect.

I think this is what is behind all the great horse-human relationships in history and I think this is a capacity **every horse and every human carries within them**. We can all have a (mutually) trusting, respectful, friendly and even loving relationship with our horses, if only we change our thinking. I know this, not because it is a sentimental dream, but because it is based on the natural laws of behavior and so, if we only go about things the right way, it **must** work. This is our automatic end result.

How to clicker train a horse

I have said several times clicker training is not a system so I don't intend to present one to you! However, I do want to show how the basic process works. If you wish to take this further there are some excellent courses and books you can read that will present you with a structure and goal-orientated path to follow. If you have already invested in a system such as natural horsemanship you could go back to it and look at the exercises again. Now that you understand the differences between negative reinforcement and positive reinforcement, you might see how these exercises could be presented to the horse in a positive way using a clicker or techniques such as modeling that I will cover soon, but first, some history.

Dogs and dolphins

Clicker training has an interesting history. It was first seriously developed in the 1960s for training dolphins. Think about the problems you might have as one of these trainers: first, you cannot use coercive methods—no halters, sticks or whips, etc. You have to find something different.

The first idea they tried was to reward the dolphin's behavior with food but this was rather "hit and miss" because by the time the dolphins got the reward, the behavior had already been completed and there was no connection between the behavior and the reward. So here was a contradiction of our the first law of behavior:

- The behavior was not linked to something the dolphins already knew or understood, or had been trained to do.

Then someone remembered the work of a Russian scientist Ivan Pavlov and his famous dogs. Very simply what Pavlov did was to notice that his dogs began to salivate in anticipation of the arrival of food. Pavlov then introduced the sound of a bell just before he fed them. After a a few repetitions (the second law), he noticed that the sound of the bell by itself was enough to start them salivating. So the bell had become a predictor of the reward. Pavlov called this behavior "classical conditioning."

- The dolphin trainers took this idea and taught the dolphins to associate the sound of a whistle with food. The dolphins learned that if they heard the whistle they could get a food reward. They also quickly learned that whatever they were doing at the time they heard the whistle would earn a reward.

- Because the classically conditioned link between the whistle and the reward became associated with whatever the dolphins were doing at the time, this is the third law of "generalizing" because this same idea applied to literally hundreds of different circumstances.

- The dolphins took this to the next stage. They learned that by repeating the activity they could "make" the trainer whistle and so get a reward. This is operant conditioning.

- One final development was that after a time, the dolphins started doing something else, they started doing *more* than they were asked. They started *offering the trainers behaviors* to see if it could get them a whistle and a reward.

- Some say they started training the trainers!

- This is positive reinforcement training and an example of the positive side-effects and consequences of using it.

- Don't forget the trainers were also getting highly rewarded as well by achieving all their training goals.

In clicker training we replace the whistle with a clicker, a simple child's toy that produces a standard metallic click sound. This is also sometimes called a *bridging signal* as it forms a bridge between the behavior and the reward, and so predicts the reward. You will now know this bridge is classical conditioning. We also use food rewards, these can be anything the horse is willing to work for, pieces of carrot or apple are fine or you can use proprietary horse rewards. Always make sure these are based on fiber and do not contain cereal or sugar. I usually carry these in a belt pouch.

The reason we use a clicker is that it is a standard sound and does not vary, this is really useful if you are working with a partner, for example, in later work you might be in the saddle and cue the horse to produce a behavior and the partner does the clicking and presents the reward from the ground.

On the other hand you could use anything as a bridging signal, it doesn't even need to be a sound.

I have a dog that was born totally deaf, she has never heard *any* sound but I can still "clicker" train her using a hand signal or a nod of the head, the important thing is that the gesture is classically conditioned to predict the reward.

The reason I prefer the clicker is that it is neutral and doesn't change as it might if you decide to use a voice cue, such as "good boy!" The problem with vocal sounds is that they can change with mood or tone of voice and also of course, if someone else wants to train the same animal they will make a completely different sound. So keep it simple for your horse and just use a clicker.

- Vocal sounds also have a slight catch to them in that we are moving into the area of anthropomorphism. I know this might come as a surprise to some but horses don't speak English, or Japanese or German or any other human language. Honestly they don't no matter how much we wish it were so!

The first steps...

- The first step is to **classically condition** the click and the reward together I do this by simply clicking then rewarding the horse with food reward. The horse quickly comes to understand that the click **predicts** the reward.

- The second step is to get the horse to perform some action that you can click. I usually start by having the horse touch my hand, I use this because law one says we must link new information to something we already know. The horse has just received a reward from my hand so if I present it again it it is very likely to reach out and touch it and that gives me something to click.

- The third step is a really important one. We need to start right from the beginning to teach the horse that it is working for the click and not the reward. In other words we need the horse to become operant as fast as possible. If we do not do this we might end up with a horse that just sees us as a resource to be mugged for food. Ideally I like to work with a partner here but it is not absolutely necessary:

  - I get the horse to touch my hand and click when I feel the touch. The partner who is standing next to me then presents the reward. Each time we repeat this (law two) my partner moves slightly away from me. In this way we quickly get a horse that walks toward me to touch my hand for a click, then goes to my partner for the reward, then comes back to repeat the behavior. In this way—right from day one—the horse understands the idea of working for a click rather than the food.

If you haven't got a handy partner it is fine, but you must spend more time on classically conditioning (or pairing as it is called) the click and the reward. The stronger the connection, the easier it is to progress.

It is likely that somewhere along the line—especially in the early stages—the horse will try to bypass the clicker and go straight for the reward. If you are working by yourself, this is your first test! The horse is giving you his first "wrong" answer and your reaction is crucial. As you know in clicker training there are no wrong answers only neutral consequences and the opportunity for the horse to get a "free go." Do not avoid the horse and certainly don't slap the horse, just try not to react at all. If we do not react, the horse will discover that the fun has stopped. At this point I might take a couple of minutes break for the horse to think about this new information and then I would return to him and start with something easy like the hand touch that he has already learned.

If you are working with a partner it is a lot easier because neither the partner or you should react. Just re-present the cue again and the horse learns that the only way to get a reward is to earn the click.

The one thing you **must not do** is give in and let the horse have a reward anyway. It may be obvious but you are reinforcing the behavior you don't want. This is an important point because it is the most common reason for slow or non-existent progress in clicker training. The problem is we *want* to give the horse a reward in the form of a treat. We *want* to do this because it is deeply emotionally rewarding for us. This is my third point about clicker training—the difference between a treat and a reward—and it is vital to understand it because if you give into your human instincts and give out a treat, suddenly the horse doesn't matter and will be confused, and you will be reinforcing the wrong behavior. You might have noticed that people who routinely treat their horses are always being mugged for food and always giving-in to their horse even at some personal risk to themselves. This is because they have "worked hard" to train the horse to do this! Clicker trainers never get mugged in this way because they only reward the behavior they want.

Copying or modeling

There is one more technique you can use which is also based on positive reinforcement called modeling or copying. In traditional education there is a lot of resistance to any notion of copying someone else. This is strange because *it is one of the most powerful, efficient and effective learning tools you can use.* Learning by imitation is totally positive; once again there are no wrong answers. Copying is based on a principle called "successive approximation" in which a behavior is imitated then compared and refined— with each repetition being closer than the last to the original. In the human world we see this when people study a foreign language, learn a musical instrument, learn to dance or participate in gymnastics and other types of sport. You never do it perfectly the first time.

We can also apply this idea to teaching our horses, and if we reward closer and closer approximations with a reinforcer such as a click and reward then we will be able to turbo charge even this powerful technique.

Some horsemen have taken the idea that horse communication is based on body language and applied the notion of modeling very effectively. One particularly good example of this is the horse trainer Klaus Ferdinand Hempfling. I believe he originally trained in drama and dance, so was very used to the idea of expressing ideas and emotions through his own body language before he realized it could be applied to horses. If you watch a video of him working with a horse you will see that both the horse and the human are imitating each other's body language. Pause the video at almost any point to see what I mean.

Imitation is something horses do all the time. Perhaps you have seen two horses galloping around the paddock, mirroring each other's body language as they turn and twist together, or if you watch horses that are "best friends," (more scientifically called pair-bonding) you will notice they spend a lot of time grazing and moving together, both facing the same direction, each imitating the behavior of the other. Even humans do this, if you watch people who are really good friends or lovers you will notice how much, quite subconsciously, they imitate each others behavior.

One of the techniques that psychologists and salesmen are taught is "mirroring"—to deliberately mimic the behavior of the other person. The reason they do this is because humans are instantly attracted to other humans who mirror our body language. Even though we may not be able to explain why it is, we instinctively like people who behave in the same way we do.

So copying the behavior of others, and, of course, having others copy your own behavior, is a powerful training technique that we can and should use with our horses. Here are some observations I made when I first saw the video of the book by Klaus Ferdinand Hempfling called *Dancing with Horses*.

KFH has the horse move around him in an outer circle as he moves on a smaller inner circle. As usual the horse and human mirror each other's body movements. Then KFH comes to a halt and tips his pelvis backwards so that he halts with his feet underneath him in perfect balance; the horse then does the same in a perfect "collected" halt. This later extends to the point KFH almost comes to a halt but carries on and the horse imitates this. In this way half-halts and collection are taught from the ground. I say, "are taught" although I doubt the horse realizes it is being taught anything. It is simply doing what is natural to the horse by imitating the body language of another.

You will notice there is no element of correction, no driving or threat. In fact, the horse is following the human, taking cues by matching the body language of his teacher. There are no negative consequences for doing this and the horse instinctively refines its behavior and tries through the use of successive approximations to reproduce that behavior more accurately. If we combine this with an emotional reward such as a click we have a really powerful training technique that we can apply in thousands of different scenarios both on the ground and from the saddle.

These are all methods we can use to build our relationship with the horse and the more we use these techniques the closer that relationship will be. You will find that your horses *want* to be trained in this way and will quickly start offering you behaviors to see if they can get rewarded. Then it is up to you which elements you pick out and develop. This is why we don't necessarily need a system to guide us because we are forging our own path as we go, letting our horse shape our teaching. Try it, it's an exciting journey!

Summary Chapter 11: Positive Reinforcement Training and Relationships

- Humans are predators; horses are prey animals.
- Any relationship must be built on the trust between them.
- Trust means trusting the other's decisions and choices.
- These decisions lead to good feelings for the horse.
- Good feelings and trust lead to respect.

- The bridge works both ways.
- Positive reinforcement training is not a system, it is a mechanism.
- Right behaviors are always rewarded because we want more of them.
- There are no wrong behaviors, only a neutral reaction or a free go.
- Clicker training basics:
  - classical conditioning
  - operant conditioning
  - the difference between a treat and a reward
- First steps of clicker training:
  - click predicts reward
  - reward response
  - separate click from reward
- Copying and modeling is another positive approach.

Chapter 12
Great Questions, Great Answers

This final chapter is in many ways the most important one because we approach the big picture, the overview. In it you will discover how the hidden horses philosophy fits with the world but before I reveal that I want to return to the one question that has puzzled me all my life and with which I started this book: "Why do otherwise nice human beings do the things they do to animals?"

The emotion of compassion

Whenever I meet pet or horse owners or any other type of "animal person," I know we share an instant, common bond. Strangely, this bond is based on the natural human instinct for anthropomorphizing animals, but in a positive way—a universal bond of the emotion of compassion. We care about what happens to animals and our compassion leads us to devote our lives to caring for their welfare. However, although compassion is our common starting point, the eventual destination of developing our personal model or belief system can be very different depending on whether our compassion leads us to take a view of animals based on **sympathy** or **empathy**.

Sympathy or empathy

These two emotions are based on two opposite points of view, leading to negative or positive results when working with animals. **Sympathy assumes an understanding while empathy seeks an understanding.** When we take our instinctive compassion and combine it with sympathy we slip down the slope of anthropomorphism and I think by now you know where that can lead. Sympathy makes us think, *You poor creature, you must be cold, frightened, hungry, helpless, alone, sad, etc. You need to be protected because if I were in your place I would feel awful!* Sympathy is based on imagining how one would feel in the same circumstances—anthropomorphism—while empathy asks the questions:

- What do I need to know about you as an animal?

- In order to understand your needs, what do I need to learn or create?

- How do you fit into the world and how can I reproduce that in terms of your environment?

- How might that benefit us both?

Empathy provides relief to the subject *as defined by the subject*, rather than provide relief to the care-giver or as defined by the care-giver.

Compassion leads the way

This mix-up in the basis of human compassion is what allows animal rescue charities to operate out of deep, heart-felt sympathy, yet rescue horses from one utility model *only to return them to another*. This is what leads dedicated, sympathetic vets and animal professionals to make diagnoses based on human medicine and recovery models which never ultimately heal the animal. And it is recognizing this paradox that leads a few of us to seek out and discover the path of empathy and understanding to reveal the *hidden horse*.

Compassion + Empathy = Natural Horse Keeping

Natural horse keeping is based on a holistic approach in which we take into consideration the whole world of the horse *as well as the human*. Let's go back to our quadrant diagram in which I've made one more modification to complete the diagram.

When we talk about a holistic approach we usually define it in four ways:

- physical

- mental

- spiritual

- emotional

These four elements fit very neatly into our finished diagram:

INCREASE	DECREASE
Reinforce/Reward	Punish
Positive Reinforcement Add something positive NATURAL HORSE KEEPING MODEL: **Feminine** Herd life, movement, choice, long-fiber diet Principles of NHK Health **EMOTIONAL**	**Positive Punishment** Add something negative UTILITY MODEL: **Masculine** Physical tools, history, tradition Practical, efficient **PHYSICAL**
Negative Reinforcement Remove something negative NATURAL HORSEMANSHIP MODEL: **Masculine** Hunting AND Training: goals, stalking, driving, ritual **MENTAL**	**Negative Punishment** Remove something positive ANTHROPOMORPHIC MODEL: **Feminine** Housing, clothing, shoeing, diet Sickness, depression **SPIRITUAL**
COMMUNICATION **Natural Horse Keeping**: positive reinforcement training, clicker training, target training, copying/modeling **Natural Horsemanship**: round pen, rope halters, sticks and strings	**CONTROL** **Utility**: bits, bridles, whips, spurs, martingales, chains, blinkers, etc. **Anthropomorphic**: stables, blankets, horseshoes, diets

- You will see that in the positive punishment quadrant we have the utility model and the **physical** world. This is where you will find all the tools of control and training and the most physical interaction between humans and horses. Sadly, this is also where you will find the most physical pain inflicted.

- Below that is the negative punishment quadrant. This is associated with the anthropomorphic ideas about stables, clothing, shoeing and diet. It is also the part of the world that affects the horse's **spirit**. This is why it is so damaging and why it it is associated with the absence of health—sickness, suffering, depression and disease.

- Both the utility and anthropomorphic quadrants are on the side of the diagram concerned with control over the horse.

- On the other side, the communication, side we have the natural horsemanship quadrant of negative reinforcement. This is the **mental** quadrant because it is all about training the horse and thus communicating with it.

- The final quadrant is the natural horse keeping area. It is the one most associated with the horse's **emotions.** It is associated with freedom of choice, good health and well-being and it is linked to the idea of a natural herd life that is in balance.

The only model that takes all the positive things I have mentioned in this book and reveals to us the hidden horse, is the natural horse keeping model. This is where the future of horses and humans must lie, and this is the understanding we must adopt for our own benefit, as well as that of our horses. This model takes nothing away from the horse adding only benefits to its world.

Final thoughts

Now you have the information you need to understand the concept of keeping horses naturally, and I hope I have opened your mind a little with a deeper understanding of these incredible animals, and what it truly means to be a horse. Indeed, what it means to *own* a horse.

I know the ideas presented in this book will represent a challenge to some readers. Many will agree with some, if not all, of what I've written, but I know they may be reluctant to make the recommended changes to their horse's environment for fear of losing something enjoyable or valued about their present relationship. I would argue this is based more on superstition than fact. To the readers who are afraid of losing good feelings, may I just say that in my experience they will not lose, but gain many, many more good feelings and experiences than they currently enjoy.

If you remember the law of positive reinforcement, you will remember that it, like all the other laws, has side effects. But unlike the other laws, these side effects are always positive. And it is these side effects that will form the basis of your new satisfaction in your relationship with your horse. This will always work because your horse will also benefit from positive side effects. Bottom line, you will both be rewarded, and you will both want more.

The chief reward you will get is that your activities with your horse will be based on building a bridge of trust. If your horse trusts you, it will like and respect you. This is the basis of a true relationship. If you continue to think anthropomorphically about your horse, your horse will **never** fully trust you. How could it?

This is why this book is called *Revealing Your Hidden Horse*, the more positives you put into your relationship, the more your hidden horse will reveal itself.

- The way to put positives into your relationship is to start to respect the horse for what it is—a brilliant, beautiful, athletic, intelligent prey animal—and to return it to the animal it was born to be.

- The more we move the horse away from its natural instincts, thoughts, feelings and emotions, the more unnatural we make the horse's life, and the more both parties will suffer. The horse will be forced to engage its natural instincts to resist our coercion, and we will be forced to devise ever more ingenious ways of preventing the horse from doing so. In this scenario, the battle between prey and predator will continue.

I hope that in this book I have shown you why this is true and how we can change it.

The world that we have built for horses throughout history and tradition is truly a dark one, with horses always on the losing side. Out actions are creating sicker, more dangerous horses with a significantly reduced life expectancy than is natural to the species. Anthropomorphism has ensured that the horse world mirrors our own, and as our collective health deteriorates, so does that of our horses—for similar reasons and through similar causes.

The hardest part of all of this is to change our thinking. Changing the physical circumstances of our horses is easy. We built the environment; we can change it. But nothing will happen until we change our beliefs and move to a better model of thinking.

Some people are born with a passion that drives them to achieve remarkable things in life, for they see the patterns and truths that others miss. For Mark Hanson a passionate interest in animals and a revelation early in life led him to a lifetime of learning and the search for a deeper perspective on both animal and human behavior. Mark Hanson grew up as the son of a veterinarian within the science of a busy London veterinary hospital to be exposed at an early age to countless examples of complex human-animal interactions. He witnessed how these relationships were defined by—and strongly biased in favor of—the humans. This became young Mark's defining discovery.

He took up a career—inevitably based around working with animals—at first in agriculture, where he learned about the many practical uses humans have for animals, then in zoological gardens. This was at a time of great change for zoos because public perception was changing. It was no longer acceptable for animals to be displayed for public amusement in dull, featureless, rectangular cages. People wanted to match the natural animal behavior they saw on their TV screens in wildlife documentaries with what they could see at a zoo, but even more importantly, the previous "unlimited" supplies of wild-caught animals consumed by zoos were rapidly diminishing. Mark realized the keys to getting people to understand the urgency of this situation were education, communication and science, and he was instrumental in communicating this to audiences of zoo visitors. Mark discovered a love and talent for communication and teaching as he presented new and exciting ideas to the public. It was also a time when his two children entered his life.

After a lifetime of caring for animals, circumstances allowed Mark to become the home parent, raise the children, and learn more about the things that interested him: languages, computers, and of course, anything to do with science and animals. This led to several part-time positions, but one was to prove especially life changing when his daughter's love for horses influenced his choice to work at a stable.

The stable had over forty horses and was run on very conventional lines with a strong emphasis on classical dressage. This rather conservative environment proved to be a major influence on the direction of Mark's life as the customs, rules and superstitions that surrounded traditional horse management dramatically conflicted with the scientific/behavioral/zoological approach. These conflicting ideas slowly began to form the foundation of the principles that would later become the Hidden Horses project.

A further influence appeared at this time as Mark became exposed to the early days of natural horsemanship in the UK. Building on his original, youthful revelation about human-animal interactions, Mark watched as others around the world started to look at the horse differently—more as a species in its own right—seeing things from the horse's point of view. This discovery heralded the next step on his path: Mark needed his own horses and a place to keep them. For that he needed money.

Pursuing his interest in computers, Mark enrolled in a higher education course with Exeter University. After graduating in computer science, he obtained a post as a college lecturer, giving him enough money to fund the next leg of his journey. With a growing herd of horses, he applied himself full-time to the study of the science behind horse behavior, embarking on a 14-module course at the Natural Animal Center (NAC) in Carmarthen in South Wales. What he learned changed his thinking forever to form the basis of many of the ideas that went into this book.

Increasingly devoting his time to equine matters, Mark now lives and works in Cornwall in the UK where he keeps a herd of four horses in accordance with the principles of natural horse keeping. He writes a blog and maintains a site at HiddenHorses.com to support the growing community built around the principles of 21st century horse keeping as he expands and applies these principles to horse training—promoting happier human-horse interactions and healthier relationships no longer biased in favor of the humans.